Live, Laugh, Cook.

Printed in The United States of America.

For information, contact Private Affairs Catering at pvtaffairs@aol.com.
Visit our website at www.pvtaffairs.com

ISBN: 0-9762430-0-8

Cover and Book Design: Leigh Maida, Philadelphia, Pennsylvania
Editing: Karen Hale Toth and Abbe Mazer Lunger
Project Management/Print Production: PrintMedia, LLC., Media, Pennsylvania

FIRST EDITION

To my husband Clint, for his never-ending and unconditional support and encouragement. Allowing me to fulfill my dreams and adventures in life. I love you!

To my children Dominick and Tina, for not letting me get away with anything, keeping me on my toes and pushing me to realize my goals.

To my parents Armando and Santina, for instilling in me a sense of independence, resilience and strength.

And to my grandbabies Christopher and Clint, for keeping me smiling and loving life even more.

Acknowledgements

I want to thank the people who have made this book possible. Thank you to family, friends and clients. Everyone played an important role.

Abbe, for her leadership and patience. Always reminding me that this was 'my book.' Tiffany, for her encouragement, insights, flexibility and hard work; typing this whole book from handwritten notes. Leigh, for taking my style and personality and making it come alive in the design. Karen, for helping to put my thoughts into words. And my clients and cooking class students, for encouraging me over the years to write this cookbook and realize this dream.

Contents

Introduction

I kind of fell into my career, yet my background had a lot to do with the tumble. I was raised in an environment where food and service are significant. Thus I started on a journey to feed everyone I could, and do it in style. I became a caterer, the ideal career for the first born daughter of an Italian family. I wasn't going to be a doctor or a lawyer, yet with food such a major part of my life, I could be the professor of parties, the woman in charge, the caterer.

I cater as though my clients are eating at my dining table with the rest of my relatives. Birthdays, holidays, communions and confirmations are held at my house. I have service for 200, along with baskets, bowls and pottery—there's enough to fill a catering hall twice over. I can cook for 200 people in a day and often do.

I have hundreds of cookbooks and magazines, and I often read them as I suspect others devour a good novel. My life is food, and with that has evolved a quest for travel and new experiences. The culinary world has broadened my horizons and I now see the world as a wonderful place to explore.

A goal I set for myself was to write a cookbook—a cookbook I, too would love to have in my kitchen—to pick up, read, grab when I needed a good, quick delicious meal, along with some inspiration and maybe a good story to put a smile on my face. A book stained with labors of love—olive oil, garlic, honey and sticky fingers.

This book is now a reality. Filled with great, easy, delicious recipes, hints and tips on food and tidbits on life—it's a book meant to be used and shared, given as a gift and cherished as your own. I hope you enjoy *Live, Laugh, Cook.* every time you have the opportunity to pick it up! And remember to cook with love, live your life with passion and don't forget a little humor goes a long way.

Bon Appetit

Susan

APPETIZERS

When displaying dips and spreads, save some key ingredients with which to garnish the dip to show your guests what is in the dip.

Roasted Red Pepper Dip

4 large roasted red peppers
2-3 cloves garlic, minced
1 tablespoon chopped Italian flat leaf parsley
3 8-ounce packages cream cheese, softened
Kosher salt and fresh cracked pepper to taste

To roast peppers, put peppers on direct flame either in your broiler, on top of your gas stove, or on your barbecue grill. Cook until charred black, turning once. When the skin is burnt black, put the peppers in a brown bag to steam and cool. Put the brown bag in a bowl so the bag won't rip open when it gets wet. When the peppers are cool enough to handle, peel off the charred skin—it should come off easily. Scrape off the seeds and cut peppers into strips. Combine in food processor with remaining ingredients. Though this is a delicious dip, the peppers by themselves are delicious tossed with garlic, olive oil, salt and pepper.

Tuscano "Cheese & Honey"

This is simply a classic Italian dish, so easy, so wonderful. Your guests will lick their fingers and come back until it's gone.

1 lb. sliced sharp Italian cheese (you can use pecorino cheese, stella fontenella cheese or sharp provolone cheese)
1⁄4 cup honey (any honey will do, but flavored honey will add zest—experiment!)

Layer cheese on platter and drizzle with honey. Be sure to provide lots of napkins. This is finger-licking good!

Spicy Olive Oil Dip

When my family comes to dinner, I make sure to have a plate of this delicious and easy dip along with plenty of Italian bread.

1 cup olive oil
1⁄4 cup balsamic vinegar
1 tablespoon chopped Italian flat leaf parsley
1 tablespoon grated Parmesan cheese
Sprinkle of red pepper flakes
Kosher salt and fresh cracked pepper to taste

In a beautiful Italian pottery dish, pour in olive oil and drizzle balsamic vinegar on top. Sprinkle remaining ingredients all over. Deceptively simple and delicious. Serve with plenty of bread for dipping.

Always use the freshest grated Parmesan or locatelli romano cheese. Purchase at a cheese store or local pasta store. You will really taste the difference!

Ricotta Cheese Spread

With Italian flavors, simple foods work best! Easy for the cook, too!

1 lb. fresh whole milk ricotta cheese
1⁄2 cup olive oil
Kosher salt and fresh cracked pepper to taste

Mound ricotta cheese in a pretty dish and drizzle with olive oil. Sprinkle with salt and pepper. To jazz this up, you can use chopped tomato or chopped olives as an extra topping. And of course, serve with bread and a wonderful glass of wine.

Growing up we had Italian bread that was delivered daily to our door step, crisp and warm from the oven. It was dense inside and had a hard crispy crust. All other brands (soft and sliced) bought in plastic was considered American bread.

Bacon and Tomato Dunk

- 10 slices bacon, cut up, cooked and drained
- 3 large tomatoes, cut up
- 1 cup mayonnaise
- 1 tablespoon Dijon mustard
- 1/4 cup chopped scallion
- 1/4 cup chopped Italian flat leaf parsley
- 4 ounces cream cheese, softened
- Dash hot pepper
- Kosher salt and fresh cracked pepper to taste

Combine all ingredients in a food processor. Reserve a few crumbles of bacon, cut up tomato and parsley for garnish. Serve with bread rounds or assorted crackers.

Bread rounds can be cut from long Italian rolls. They are the right size for spreads, hors d'oeuvres, and croutons.

Cream Cheese with Rustic Salsa

This will disappear fast.

- 2 8-ounce packages cream cheese
- 6 plum tomatoes, chopped
- 1 cup chopped red onion
- 1 4.5-ounce can chopped green chili
- 1 tablespoon chopped Italian flat leaf parsley
- 2 cloves garlic, minced
- 1/4 cup olive oil
- 1 teaspoon lime juice
- Kosher salt and fresh cracked pepper to taste

Cut cream cheese into slices and layer in a pretty pottery dish. Combine remaining ingredients and pour over cream cheese. Serve cold with tortilla chips, bread slices or crackers.

In a pinch, you can use red onion as a substitute for any recipe with onion as an ingredient. Red onions have a sweet, subtle flavor and are delicious!

We cook with all of our senses. Our hands can tell us the right texture, our eyes can determine doneness and taste can adjust seasonings. We listen for the sizzling of a steak. Our noses play an especially important part. As foods cook we can smell the fragrance of aromas mingling. When we smell a roast cooking or brownies baking—BETTER GO CHECK THEM—they are almost done!

Salmon Mousse

- 2 8-ounce packages cream cheese, softened
- 1/4 cup heavy cream
- 2 scallions, chopped
- 1 teaspoon lemon juice
- Dash hot sauce
- 6 ounces smoked salmon
- Kosher salt and fresh cracked pepper to taste

In food processor, chop salmon coarsely with the pulse button. Remove and set aside. Do not clean processor. Put in remaining ingredients and blend until smooth. Fold in the chopped salmon by hand. You can serve this in a hollowed out bread loaf, with bagel slices, on a pretty dish, or piped onto cucumber rounds. Garnish with tiny capers or caviar.

Treat yourself to the best ingredients available. You are worth it! Whatever you put into your cooking will shine through when your meal is ready to be served.

THE FISHING ROD

At some point in our lives, we become responsible for ourselves. Before that, we have a tendency to think parents should provide for us, their children, in every way. This was true for me as I was growing up. Fortunately for me, my father had different beliefs. Coming from hard work all his life, his ideas about raising me were to 'teach me to fish,' figuratively speaking that is.

My father believed that if I learned how to make a living, using my own money for things I wanted and craved, I would be set for life. Of course, I disagreed with him at the time, but have since realized that he was absolutely right all along! It seems that as I was growing up, I was always asking for the fish instead of asking for a lesson on how to catch them myself.

Today, I am a very independent woman. I can support myself and my kids, and I enjoy life and the gratification of earning my own living. Sometimes, though, when I'm tired and overworked, I do wish Dad would throw some fish my way!

Sante Fe Dip

This is one of my most requested recipes.

2 cups shredded orange cheddar cheese
1 cup shredded Monterrey Jack cheese
1⁄2 cup mayonnaise
1 4.5-ounce can chopped green chili
1 teaspoon hot sauce
1 cup frozen corn, defrosted
Kosher salt and fresh cracked pepper to taste

Mix together ingredients. Put in ovenproof pottery dish and garnish with topping. Bake uncovered at 350º for 20-25 minutes. Serve with crackers or bread slices. This will disappear fast!

Topping

2 plum tomatoes, chopped
1⁄4 cup chopped scallions
2 tablespoons chopped fresh cilantro or Italian flat leaf parsley

Hot Crab & Cheese Dip

2 tablespoons butter, melted
2 scallions, cut up
1⁄2 pepper, chopped
1⁄3 cup chopped tomato
1 10-ounce can cheddar cheese soup
1⁄3 cup light cream
1 teaspoon lemon juice
Dash hot sauce
1⁄2 cup shredded cheddar cheese
1 lb. jumbo lump crabmeat
Kosher salt and fresh cracked pepper to taste

Sauté scallions, pepper and tomato in butter. Season with salt and pepper. Add all remaining ingredients except crabmeat. Stir 5-10 minutes until blended. Fold in crabmeat. Pour into casserole dish and sprinkle with paprika. Bake uncovered at 350º for 35-40 minutes until golden. Serve with bread slices, crackers or celery sticks.

Feta Salsa

A fun and delicious recipe.

1 pound feta cheese, crumbled
1 cup olive oil
6 scallions, minced
1⁄2 cup minced Italian flat leaf parsley
4 large tomatoes, chopped
1 tablespoon lime juice
1 teaspoon dried oregano
1 teaspoon dried dill
Kosher salt and fresh cracked pepper to taste

Mix and serve with pita bread or tortilla chips. Do not use a food processor for this, mix by hand. This recipe can be made up to one day ahead.

If using dry herbs instead of fresh use half the amount. Dry herbs are more concentrated.

Chopped green chili can be found in the supermarket aisle that displays salsa and taco mix. It is a mild chili and not hot at all.

Assorted Brie

Instead of an ordinary cheese board, I love to use a baked brie as a cheese display. The brie always disappears! Here are several ideas. Be sure to place brie in a pretty ovenproof pottery dish to bake because it is nearly impossible to transfer.

Praline Brie

1 large wheel of brie with rind intact (about 12 inches)
1 stick butter, melted
1 1⁄2 cups brown sugar
1 1⁄2 cups chopped pecans

Melt butter. Add brown sugar. Turn off heat. Add nuts. Stir well. Pour mixture on top of brie. (Can be made ahead to this point.) When ready to serve, bake uncovered at 350º for 15-20 minutes. The brie will be soft and gooey and the nuts delicious! Serve warm with bread slices.

Store large quantities of nuts in the freezer to keep them fresh longer.

Candied Cranberry and Orange Brie

Colorful and delicious for the holidays.

1 large wheel of brie with rind intact (about 12 inches)
2 12-ounce bags whole fresh cranberries, rinsed
2 cups sugar
1⁄4 cup triple sec
1⁄4 cup orange juice
1 11-ounce can mandarin orange slices with syrup (use 1⁄4 cup syrup)

In saucepan, combine fresh cranberries, sugar, triple sec and orange juice over medium heat. Cook for 20 minutes. Cranberries will burst. Remove from heat and let cool. Stir in mandarin orange slices and syrup. Top brie and bake uncovered in a 350º oven for 15-20 minutes. Serve warm with bread slices or crackers.

Baked Brie with Fig Preserve and Sugared Nuts

1 large wheel of brie with rind intact (about 12 inches)
1 8-ounce jar fig preserve (or blueberry, strawberry or raspberry)

Sugared Nuts

1 stick butter, melted
1 1⁄2 cups brown sugar
1 1⁄2 cups any kind of nuts (walnuts, sliced almonds, pecans, macadamia)

Melt butter. Add brown sugar. Turn off heat. Add nuts. Stir well. Top brie with jar of fruit preserves then top with nuts. Heat uncovered at 350º for 15-20 minutes. Serve warm with bread slices or crackers.

Baked Garlic with Brie

1 cup peeled garlic
1⁄2 cup olive oil
Kosher salt and fresh cracked pepper to taste
2 tablespoons fresh rosemary
Slices of Italian Rolls
1 lb. of brie, sliced

In sauté pan, cook garlic in oil with salt, pepper and rosemary on high heat until mixture starts to bubble on the sides. Lower heat and simmer, stirring occasionally until garlic is soft and golden. Spoon some garlic cloves on top of bread slices and then put slice of brie on top. Bake uncovered at 350º for 10 minutes or until brie melts.

This garlic mixture can also be puréed in a food processor with 8 ounces cream cheese to make a wonderful smokey and nutty flavored spread.

Assorted Bruschetta

It's always fun to offer a variety of flavors. I love to set out a bruschetta table with colorful bowls of different toppings and a big basket of bread slices in the center.

Roasted Grape Tomato Bruschetta

2 pints grape tomatoes, rinsed
2 cloves garlic, minced
1⁄4 cup finely chopped shallot or red onion
4 tablespoons olive oil
1 tablespoon sugar (can use brown sugar)
Kosher salt and fresh cracked pepper to taste
1 cup grated Parmesan cheese
1⁄2 cup shredded basil

Toss all ingredients together. Put on a baking sheet sprayed with cooking spray. Roast uncovered at 350º for 30-40 minutes or until tomatoes pop. Stir once or twice during cooking. Remove from oven and stir in Parmesan cheese and basil. Serve with bread slices.

PERCEPTIONS

I've decided that life is about perceptions. Everyone has a different view on each and every situation. We each see things, people and events in a different way. We are influenced by our backgrounds, our moods, our finances, our family—truly a million things! As I go through my life, I realize that there is a reason for chocolate and vanilla—it's a choice to make. Sometimes we can't control what happens to us, but we can surely control our reaction to it. We can choose to see life with a sense of wonder and enjoyment.

With a smile and a kind word, with understanding of another person, we can take lemons and make lemon gelato! Try it, it's much more fun!

Italian White Bean Pate

This is so delicious your guests won't know they are eating beans!

1 40 1⁄2-ounce can white beans, rinsed well
1 teaspoon dried thyme
2 scallions, chopped
3 tablespoons olive oil
1 clove garlic, minced or 3-4 carmelized cloves
Kosher salt and fresh cracked pepper to taste

Combine all ingredients in a food processor until blended. Reserve some beans and scallion for garnish.

To easily carmelize garlic:

1 cup peeled garlic cloves
1⁄2 cup olive oil
Kosher salt and fresh cracked pepper to taste

In a sauté pan, cook garlic over high heat for 5 minutes until oil gets hot. Reduce heat and simmer. Stir occasionally until garlic gets soft and golden. Cool and keep in the refrigerator for up to two weeks.

To cut basil without bruising, layer leaves on top of one another and then roll into a log. With a sharp knife, cut the logs into strips. You will immediately smell the fresh fragrance.

Fettunta

A wonderful bruschetta that I first tasted in a winery in Tuscany.

4 scallions, chopped
1 cup shredded arugula
1⁄2 cup olive oil
1⁄4 cup grated Parmesan cheese
Kosher salt and fresh cracked pepper to taste
Toasted Italian bread slices

Combine scallion, arugula, salt, pepper, olive oil and cheese. Spoon on toasted bread slices. Deliciously different!

Artichoke and Ricotta Bruschetta

1⁄2 cup artichoke hearts, drained
1 cup whole milk ricotta cheese
2 cloves garlic, chopped
1⁄2 cup grated Parmesan cheese
Kosher salt and fresh cracked pepper to taste

Combine ingredients in food processor. Be sure to reserve an artichoke for garnish so that guests will know what they are eating!

Olive Tapenade

1 cup stuffed green olives
1 cup black pitted olives
1⁄2 cup capers
2 cloves garlic, minced
1⁄4 cup chopped Italian flat leaf parsley
1⁄2 cup olive oil
1 anchovy
Fresh cracked pepper to taste

Combine ingredients in a food processor. Use the pulse button and keep this mixture chunky.

Party Pointers

- Do your shopping early and make lists.
- Plan your menu. Don't use all new recipes.
- Take out all the serving pieces, clean and polish at least a week before.
- Use luminaries to light the way to the door. It's festive and fun and adds a glowing path of light to your party.
- Keep drinks at one end of the house and food at the other to avoid congestion.
- Use cut up vegetables as well as bread sticks, bread slices or cubes and chips for dipping.
- Serve dip in hollowed-out breads or red and green peppers for a festive look.
- Serve plenty of room temperature food.
- Offer little plates and plenty of napkins, even if serving finger foods.

Shrimp Wrapped in Bacon with Horseradish Sauce

2 lbs. cooked and cleaned shrimp
1 lb. bacon

Cut bacon slices in thirds. Wrap shrimp with bacon. Bake uncovered on a greased cookie sheet at 350º until crisp, 15-20 minutes.

Horseradish Sauce

1 cup mayonnaise
1⁄4 cup horseradish
1 tablespoon chopped Italian flat leaf parsley
Fresh cracked pepper to taste
1 teaspoon ketchup

Combine ingredients in bowl and refrigerate until serving.

Care for Your Cut Flowers

- Use a few drops of bleach in water or add an aspirin to prevent flowers from fading.
- Keep flowers in a bright, but cool area.
- Re-cut stems on a slant and remove leaves that wilt below water line.
- Change water daily.
- Choose a vase that is about half as tall as your flowers.
- Drop a penny into the water in a vase to keep tulips from drooping.

"New Orleans Style" Barbecue Sauce

3 lbs. cooked and cleaned shrimp
3 tablespoons olive oil
6 cloves garlic, minced
2 teaspoons red pepper flakes
1 tablespoon Worcestershire sauce
1 teaspoon dried thyme
2 teaspoons paprika
1 teaspoon dried oregano
Kosher salt and fresh cracked pepper to taste
1 tablespoon hot sauce
1 tablespoon brown sugar
1⁄4 cup ketchup
1⁄2 cup chopped scallion

Add all ingredients to hot oil except shrimp and scallion. Cook for 10 minutes until fragrant. Toss with shrimp. Sprinkle with scallion and serve.

Rum Runner Shrimp

5 lbs. cooked and cleaned shrimp
3 tablespoons olive oil
1 cup chopped onion
3 cloves garlic, minced
1 cup ketchup
1⁄3 cup red wine vinegar
2 tablespoons Worcestershire sauce
1⁄2 cup rum
1 tablespoon honey
Dash hot sauce
1 teaspoon paprika

Sauté onion and garlic in hot oil for 5 minutes. Add remaining ingredients (except shrimp) and cook 10-15 minutes. Toss with shrimp. Serve hot or cold.

Cheddar Stuffed Mushrooms

1 1/2 lbs. mushrooms, stems removed & chopped
4 tablespoons butter, melted
1 cup chopped onion
Kosher salt and fresh cracked pepper to taste
1/2 cup chopped Italian flat leaf parsley
1 1/2 cups shredded cheddar cheese
1 cup fresh bread crumbs

Sauté chopped mushroom stems and onion in butter. Season with salt and pepper. Cook until soft 10-15 minutes. Toss with parsley, cheese and bread crumbs. Stuff mushroom caps and place on an ovenproof pottery platter. Bake uncovered at 350º for 15-20 minutes.

Blue Cheese Stuffed Mushrooms

1 1/2 lbs. mushrooms, stems removed & chopped
3 tablespoons butter, melted
2 cloves garlic, minced
Kosher salt and fresh cracked pepper
1/2 cup chopped scallions
1 cup crumbled blue cheese
1 cup fresh bread crumbs

Sauté chopped mushroom stems and garlic in butter. Season with salt and pepper. Mix with scallion, blue cheese and bread crumbs. Stuff mushroom caps. Place in an ovenproof pottery dish and bake uncovered at 350º for 15-20 minutes.

Clean mushrooms with a mushroom brush or paper towel. Never submerge in water. Mushrooms are like little sponges and quickly soak up water, which dilutes the taste and makes for a soggy mushroom.

Fry Me a River

- When frying, never use olive oil—it smokes with high heat. Instead, use a blended oil.
- Heat an empty frying pan first, then add the oil. It will heat up quickly and evenly. You should hear a sizzle when the food hits the oil.
- When a recipe calls for ground mix, use a combination of beef, pork and veal for a tasty mixture.
- When frying meatballs make sure the oil is hot. Add meatballs and let brown on one side before turning. It will take less than half the time to brown the other side. Shake pan back and forth on stove to turn meatballs easily.

Spicy Chinese Meatballs

1 cup soy sauce
1/2 cup water
1/2 cup pineapple juice
1/2 cup brown sugar
1/2 cup chopped scallions
1 teaspoon chopped ginger
1 teaspoon red pepper flakes
1 tablespoon sesame oil
1 tablespoon olive oil
1 teaspoon chopped garlic

Sauté ginger and garlic in hot oil. Add remaining ingredients and cook 10-15 minutes until thick. Can be made ahead and reheated when needed.

Meatballs

2 lbs. ground mix (beef, pork and veal)
1 cup fresh bread crumbs
Kosher salt and fresh cracked pepper to taste
1 teaspoon chopped garlic
2 eggs
1 cup vegetable oil for frying

Mix all ingredients well. Roll into mini balls. Fry in oil until brown. Top meatballs with heated sauce and serve.

Jamaican Jerk Meatballs

This sauce can be used for chicken or pork skewers.

Jerk Sauce

3 tablespoons olive oil
1 teaspoon chopped garlic
1 teaspoon ground allspice
1 teaspoon ground cinnamon
1 teaspoon ground nutmeg
1 4.5-ounce can chopped green chili
Kosher salt and fresh cracked pepper to taste
1⁄4 cup red wine vinegar
1⁄4 cup soy sauce
1⁄2 cup ketchup

Sauté garlic in oil. Add remaining ingredients and cook 15-20 minutes.

Meatballs

2 lbs. ground mix (beef, pork and veal)
2 eggs
Dash hot sauce
Kosher salt and fresh cracked pepper to taste
1 cup fresh bread crumbs
1 cup vegetable oil for frying

Mix all ingredients well. Roll into mini balls. Fry in oil until brown. Top meatballs with sauce and serve.

Crab Puffs

1 lb. jumbo lump crabmeat
1⁄2 cup grated Parmesan cheese
1⁄2 cup mayonnaise
3 scallions, chopped
1 teaspoon Old Bay seasoning
1 tablespoon Dijon mustard
Dash hot sauce
Bread slices cut from long rolls

Mix all ingredients and top bread rounds with mixture. Bake uncovered at 350º for 10-15 minutes until golden.

Appealing Presentation, Popular Food

- Wrap your napkins with a twig of fresh rosemary.
- Lightly butter, then dust the rim of your platter with a colorful spice such as paprika (red) or turmeric (yellow).
- Serve crudité (fresh cut up vegetables for dip) in a group of terra cotta pots along with seasonal greens and berries.
- Tuck sprigs of cedar or pine and berries along with red or white flowers into hollowed-out artichokes.
- Use a gold tip magic marker to write names on leaves to use as place settings.

Olive Onion Puffs

1 cup chopped black olives
1⁄2 cup grated Parmesan cheese
1⁄2 cup mayonnaise
3 scallions, chopped
1⁄2 cup finely chopped onion
Kosher salt and fresh cracked pepper to taste
Bread slices cut from long rolls

Combine all ingredients and top bread rounds. Bake uncovered at 350º for 10-15 minutes until browned.

When preparing "puff" hors d'oeuvres ahead of time, bake them only 5-10 minutes and then remove from oven. They can be frozen or refrigerated and then at party time defrosted and baked an additional 5-10 minutes until brown.

"Jump in Your Lap" Chicken Skewers

2 cloves garlic, minced
1 teaspoon hot chili paste
1 tablespoon chili sauce
1 tablespoon sesame oil
1 tablespoon brown sugar
2 scallions, chopped
1/4 cup chicken broth
4 tablespoons soy sauce
1 lb. boneless chicken breast sliced into strips
6-inch bamboo skewers

Combine all ingredients except chicken and simmer for 10-15 minutes.

Thread chicken strips on bamboo skewers. Layer on cookie sheet and bake uncovered at 350º for 15-20 minutes. Remove and set aside. When ready to serve, dip cooked chicken skewers into sauce and reheat covered at 350º for 10-15 minutes.

Chicken can be prepared in advance.

Smoked Salmon and Chevre Pizza

8 ounces goat cheese
6 tablespoons sour cream
3 teaspoons horseradish
6 ounces smoked salmon, cut into strips
2 pre-cooked pizza shells
1/2 cup chopped scallion or chives

Combine goat cheese, sour cream and horseradish. Spread on pizza crust. Drape salmon on top. Bake uncovered at 350º for 10-15 minutes. Sprinkle with cut up chives or scallions. Serve in wedges.

APPROACH LOVE AND YOUR KITCHEN WITH WANTON ABANDONMENT

On one of our "Taste of Tuscany" cooking tours, Clint and I were on our way out of the walled city of Sienna when we spotted a book restorer. We happened upon the Scottish shop owner blowing the dust off of a 500-year-old book. Intrigued, we stepped into her store and discovered a jewel.

Filled with restored books dating back hundreds of years, the shop was fascinating to explore. Clint found a beautifully restored parchment with an inscription, in Italian, "Approach Love and Your Kitchen with Wanton Abandonment."

Now in my office, that parchment's inscription inspires me each time I pass by.

Chicken Satay

Satay Sauce

2 tablespoons butter
1 teaspoon sesame oil
2 cloves garlic, minced
1 teaspoon chopped ginger
1 tablespoon brown sugar
1/3 cup peanut butter
3 tablespoons ketchup
3 tablespoons soy sauce
1 teaspoon lime juice
Dash hot sauce
1/3 cup half & half
1 lb. boneless chicken breast, cut up into strips
6-inch bamboo skewers

Melt butter and sesame oil. Sauté garlic and ginger until fragrant. Add remaining ingredients (except half & half) and whisk together for 10-15 minutes until smooth. Add half & half.

Thread chicken strips on skewers. Layer on cookie sheet and bake uncovered at 350º for 15-20 minutes. Remove and set aside. When ready to serve, dip cooked chicken skewers into Satay Sauce and reheat covered at 350º for 10-15 minutes.

To keep frozen spinach from getting bitter, defrost it and rinse well before using in a recipe.

Blue Cheese Bites

2 packages refrigerated biscuits cut in quarters

1 stick butter, melted

1 cup crumbled blue cheese

Spray ovenproof pottery dish with cooking spray. Layer cut up biscuits closely together; they can touch. Mix butter and cheese and pour on top of biscuits. Bake uncovered at 350º for 15-20 minutes until golden.

Create with Candles

Candles symbolize celebration, romance and ceremony.

- Before a party, light and extinguish the candles—they'll light quicker and easier later.
- Candles refrigerated before using will burn more slowly and evenly. Wrap in foil to prevent wicks from absorbing moisture.
- When blowing out a candle, hold your finger in front of the flame and blow at it. This will prevent hot wax from splattering.
- Votive candles will clean easily if you add a few drops of water to the bottom of each glass.
- Avoid scented candles on the food table—it will interfere with food flavors.

Always buy fresh sun-dried tomatoes. Store them in the freezer. When ready to use, cover with boiling water for 5 minutes to soften. Drain water and chop.

Goat Cheese and Spinach Tarts

You can also use this as a hot dip—just skip the tart shells.

1 tablespoon olive oil

1⁄2 cup diced red onion

2 cloves garlic, minced

2 10-ounce boxes frozen chopped spinach; defrosted, rinsed and squeezed dry

8 ounces goat cheese

1⁄3 cup pine nuts

3 tablespoons grated Parmesan cheese

Kosher salt and fresh cracked pepper to taste

2-3 packages phyllo dough tart shells (available in frozen food section of supermarket)

Sauté red onion and garlic in hot oil. Add spinach, goat cheese, pine nuts and cheese. Season with salt and pepper. Fill tart shells and bake uncovered at 350º for 10-12 minutes.

When making this ahead of time, always bake tarts for at least 8-10 minutes to set. Freeze and reheat later.

Sun-Dried Tomato Tarts

2 tablespoons olive oil

1 teaspoon chopped garlic

3⁄4 cup chopped sun-dried tomatoes

Pinch dried thyme

Kosher salt and fresh cracked pepper to taste

8 ounces goat cheese

8 ounces cream cheese

3 large eggs, beaten

1⁄2 cup grated Parmesan cheese

2-3 packages phyllo dough tart shells (available in frozen food section of market)

Sauté garlic and sun-dried tomatoes in hot oil. Season with salt, pepper and thyme. Add goat cheese and cream cheese. Blend until soft. Remove from heat. Add eggs and Parmesan. Fill tart shells and bake uncovered at 350º for 10-15 minutes.

DO AHEAD TIP >> *reduce baking time to 10 minutes. Cool. Store in refrigerator. Reheat just before serving.*

Toasted Blue Cheese and Carmelized Onion Crostini

2-3 tablespoons butter, melted
2 large yellow onions, sliced thin
1 tablespoon brown sugar
Kosher salt and fresh cracked pepper to taste
Bread slices cut from long rolls
1 cup crumbled blue cheese
Chopped Italian flat leaf parsley for garnish

Sauté onions with brown sugar in butter until golden. Season with salt and pepper. This will take at least 20 minutes. Cover the onions for the first 5 minutes to "sweat them".Uncover and turn up the heat. *When they start to stick to the sides of the pan stir frequently—they are almost done!*

Top bread slices with onion mixture. Sprinkle with cheese and parsley. Bake uncovered at 350º for 10-15 minutes.

I always use Italian flat leaf parsley. It has a wonderful flavor, lots of nutrition and it's Italian! So much better than dried parsley from a bag or jar.

When having an open house or cocktail party, it is important to have some food set around so guests can help themselves. Present the foods at different heights to make the displays inviting. Be sure to place napkins and plates at each station.

Open-Faced Ham Sandwiches with Dijon Brie Spread

1 lb. brie, room temperature
1⁄4 cup Dijon mustard
Dash hot sauce
1 scallion, chopped
2 tablespoons butter, softened
Bread slices cut from long rolls
1 lb. Tavern style ham, sliced thin (You can buy this in the deli section of your supermarket. This is also a delicious way to use ham left over from a holiday meal.)

Combine brie, Dijon, hot sauce, scallion and butter in food processor until smooth. Spread on bread slices. Top with ham slices. Bake uncovered at 350º for 10-15 minutes.

Use the brie; rind and all.

Feel free to experiment with different mustards. Coarse grain, champagne and tarragon each add a wonderful flavor to most every recipe.

When incorporating butter into a mixture in cooking (not baking), always bring to room temperature first.

PIECES OF LIFE

Photographs are stories of life. Moments captured, memories relived. My house is full of photos; every wall tells a story. Beautifully framed, these jewels are constant reminders of special times, frozen for me to enjoy again and again.

Clint is my photographer. For the more than 20 years I've known him he has had a camera in hand, at the ready to capture that smile, that sunset, the colors of a NASCAR race or me with one of those drivers!

Our life is chronicled in pictures, glorious colors, special moments with our children, parents, grandchildren, neighbors, celebrations and seasons. On Halloween, we sit on the porch, me with my basket of candy and Clint with his camera. He snaps away at parents and children alike. Witches, ghosts, Dorothy from the Wizard of Oz, clowns and goblins are all photographed. The parents pick up these Halloween mementos a few weeks later, complements of Clint.

Clint is often the "staff" photographer in my cooking class for kids, capturing the little chefs whipping up their favorite food, their aprons and fingers smeared in chocolate.

Our fridge is covered with photos of family. Everywhere I look, memories. What a wonderful wallpaper of life. Take pictures. Preserve that smile for all eternity. Savor that special sunset again and again. Set those pictures in frames and put them on the wall, on your desk. Don't hide them away. With photographs you can relive each moment of happiness and joy. Life is all about family, friends and experiences to treasure and remember.

Spicy Shrimp with Raspberry Dipping Sauce

- 2 lbs. cooked and cleaned shrimp
- 2 tablespoons olive oil
- 2 cloves garlic, minced
- 1 teaspoon hot pepper flakes
- 1 teaspoon Old Bay seasoning

Sauté garlic in hot oil. Add remaining ingredients. Toss with shrimp.

Raspberry Sauce

- 1⁄2 cup raspberry preserves
- 1-2 tablespoons horseradish (or to taste)

Combine and use as a different kind of dipping sauce for shrimp. I also use cocktail sauce for those who are not adventurous.

Shrimp Wrapped in Snow Peas with Wasabi Aioli Dipping Sauce

- 1 lb. cooked and cleaned shrimp
- 1 10-ounce bag frozen snow peas, defrosted
- 1 tablespoon wasabi powder
- 2 tablespoons water
- 1 cup mayonnaise
- Kosher salt to taste

Wrap the snow peas around shrimp and secure with a tooth pick. Mix wasabi powder with water until it forms a paste. Whisk with mayonnaise and salt. Use as a dipping sauce.

Wasabi is a Japanese horseradish sold in powder form. When mixed with water it forms a paste. It is very HOT.

Tomato and Mozzarella Skewers in a Basil Marinade

1 lb. mozzarella balls

1 lb. grape tomatoes

Basil Marinade

6 tablespoons chopped basil

1⁄2 cup olive oil

1⁄4 cup grated Parmesan cheese

Kosher salt and fresh cracked pepper to taste

Combine mixture for marinade and toss with grape tomatoes and mozzarella. Skewer one tomato and one mozzarella ball. Arrange on a platter and garnish with fresh basil.

Mozzarella balls can be found in the gourmet cheese section of your supermarket. They are called Ciligene.

I love the small grape tomatoes—they are so full of flavor. In a pinch you can use cherry tomatoes or cut up plum tomatoes.

Spicy Shrimp Wasabi

3 lbs. cooked and cleaned shrimp

1-2 tablespoons olive oil

2 cloves garlic, minced

1 tablespoon wasabi powder

1 tablespoon water

Dash hot sauce

Kosher salt and fresh cracked pepper to taste

1⁄2 cup chopped scallion

Briefly soften garlic in hot oil. Mix wasabi powder with water until it forms a paste. Add oil, hot sauce, season with salt and pepper and toss with shrimp. Garnish with scallion. Serve cold.

Asparagus with Two Dipping Sauces

To check if asparagus is cooked, slice off a piece at the root end and taste it.

3 lbs. asparagus

Trim asparagus. Boil or steam for 7-8 minutes. Let cool. Display cooked asparagus standing up in a pretty pottery dish with both dipping sauces below.

Oriental Mayonnaise

2 cloves garlic, chopped

1 tablespoon chopped ginger

1⁄4 cup soy sauce

2 tablespoons brown sugar or honey

1 teaspoon sesame oil

Dash hot sauce

2 cups mayonnaise

Kosher salt and fresh cracked pepper to taste

Combine all ingredients in a food processor.

Roasted Red Pepper Dipping Sauce

2 cloves garlic, minced

1 tablespoon olive oil

Kosher salt and fresh cracked pepper to taste

2 tablespoons chopped Italian flat leaf parsley

1⁄2 cup roasted red peppers

2 cups mayonnaise

Combine all ingredients in a food processor.

SET GOALS FOR YOURSELF!
If you don't know where you are going...
you'll end up somewhere else.

Thirty Second Stress Busters

- *Open a window or walk outside to get some fresh air.*
- *Drink a whole glass of water without stopping, letting the cooling liquid sooth your tension.*
- *Take a deep breath through your nose and exhale through your mouth as if you are blowing out a candle.*
- *Sip a glass of skim milk. It contains tryptophan, an amino acid that helps promote relaxation.*
- *Stretch your arms overhead and reach as far as you can while standing on your toes.*

KEEP "QUALITY" IN YOUR LIFE

What have you done recently just for fun? When was the last time you got away for three days just for pleasure? When was the last time you said, "This day is for me. I'm going for a long walk or massage." Make time for friends. Make time for you. Take a nap—even a short one!

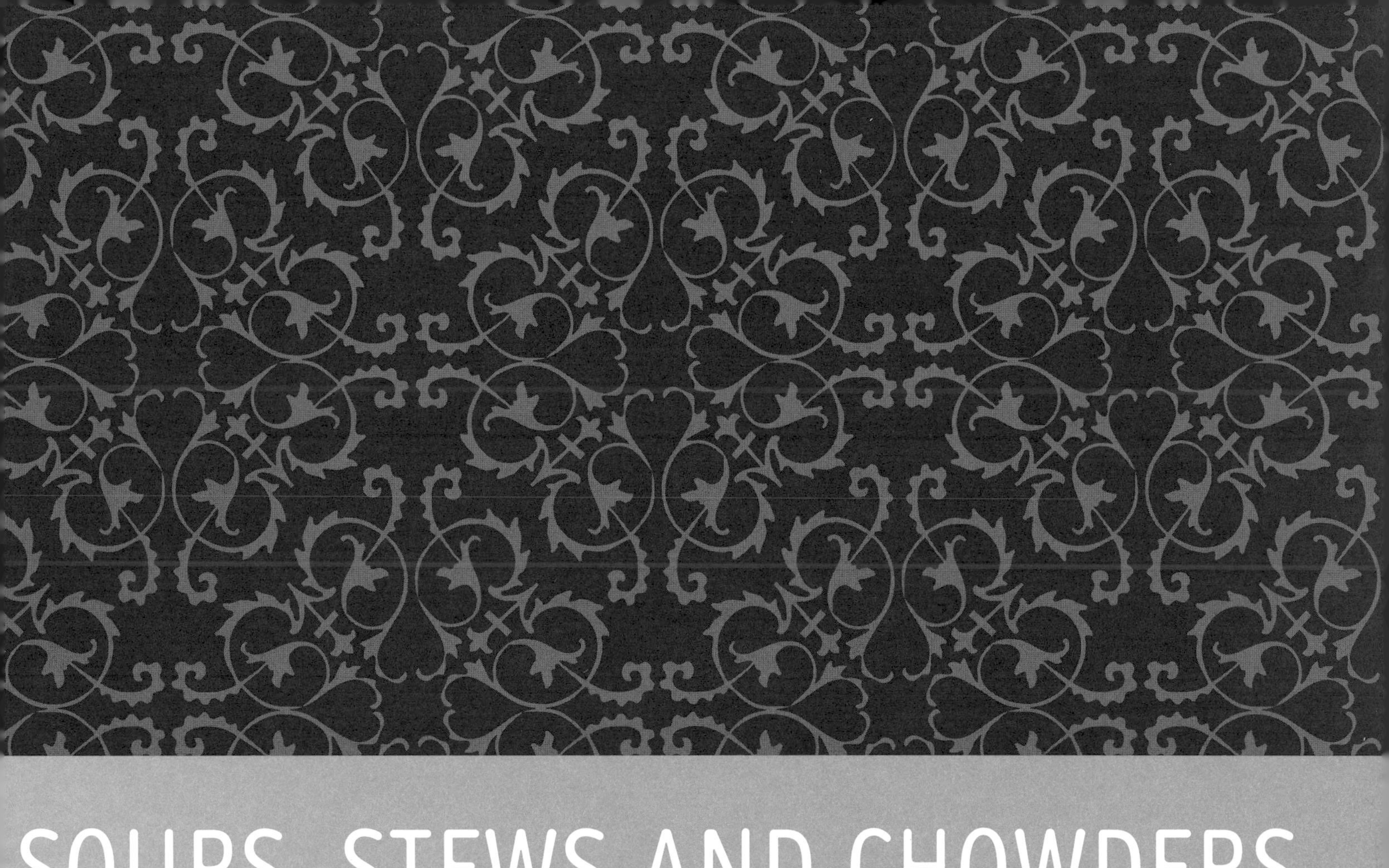

SOUPS, STEWS AND CHOWDERS

FRIENDS

Friends. This one word has so many meanings. We have casual acquaintances as well as close friends to whom we can reveal our soul. Each of these people plays an important part in our lives. Each has a purpose.

Sometimes we would like to think we could get along by ourselves...but this is certainly not true. We would miss waving hello to our neighbors in the early morning as we go outside to pick up our paper. We would miss gesturing to a familiar face in the crowd, or letting someone hug us when there are fears or sadness present in our lives. And who would we call to share some happiness or gossip?

Friends. People who are not necessarily family, but for whom we hold a very special place in our hearts. They are important to us, just as important as the air we breathe and the food we eat.

Look around. Call a friend. Be a friend. What you give today in friendship will be returned to you a thousand times over!

Key West Cuban Black Bean Soup

2 tablespoons butter, melted
1 large onion, chopped
1 pepper, diced*
2 cloves garlic, chopped
1/2 cup chopped scallion
Kosher salt and fresh cracked pepper
2 15-ounce cans black beans, rinsed
6 cups chicken broth
1 cup cooked rice
1 15-ounce can Mexican-style stewed tomatoes
1 4.5-ounce can chopped green chili

Sauté onion, pepper, garlic and scallion in butter until soft. Season with salt and pepper. Add remaining ingredients and simmer 35-45 minutes. Garnish bowl of soup with crushed tortilla chips and grated cheddar.

**Red and yellow peppers are sweeter than green peppers.*

Delicious Beef and Cabbage Soup

9 tablespoons olive oil
1 1/2 cups chopped onion
2 cups chopped carrots
6 stalks celery, chopped
4 cloves garlic, chopped
Kosher salt and fresh cracked pepper
1 teaspoon celery seed
1 head savoy cabbage, washed and chopped
1 1/2 cups chopped potato, skin on
2 lbs. beef stew, browned
2 cups marinara sauce
1 tablespoon Worcestershire sauce
1 tablespoon soy sauce
2 tablespoons brown sugar
Dash hot sauce
1 48-ounce can chicken broth

Sauté onions, carrots, celery and garlic in 6 tablespoons hot oil until fragrant. Season with salt and pepper. Add cabbage and potatoes. Cook until cabbage steams, stirring frequently. Brown beef in 3 tablespoons oil. Drain. Add beef to vegetables. Add remaining ingredients. Cover and simmer 1 to 2 hours.

Creamy Wild Mushroom Soup with Crabmeat

6 tablespoons butter, melted
3.5 ounces oyster mushrooms, sliced
3.5 ounces shiitake mushrooms, sliced
10 ounces Portabella mushrooms, sliced
10 ounces Button mushrooms, sliced
1 1⁄2 cups chopped onion
1⁄2 cup chopped Italian flat leaf parsley
Kosher salt and fresh cracked pepper to taste
1⁄3 cup flour
1 lb. jumbo lump crabmeat
1⁄2 cup light cream (optional)
2 48-ounce cans chicken broth
1⁄2 cup chopped scallions

Sauté mushrooms with onion and parsley in butter. Season with salt and pepper. Cook until limp. Add flour. Stir until flour becomes incorporated then add remaining ingredients. Simmer 25-30 minutes. You can add light cream last. Serve with carmelized mushroom garnish.

Carmelized Mushroom Garnish

2 cups mushrooms, sliced thin
2 tablespoons butter, melted
Kosher salt and fresh cracked pepper to taste

In large sauté pan, cook mushrooms in butter over high heat. Season with salt and pepper and sauté until brown. Stir occasionally.

When carmelizing mushrooms, cook over high heat. Do not crowd in sauté pan. Steam rising from the bottom layer will make mushrooms soft instead of carmelized.

Give Salt A Fair Shake

- Sea salt is rich in minerals.
- English sea salt has a very salty taste and large flakes.
- Brittany sea salt is from northern France, grayish in color and delicate in flavor.
- Fleur de Sel, "Flower of Salt," is from salt marshes in France.
- Kosher salt is a purified and high-grade crystal rock salt with a coarseness that's ideal for cooking.
- Table salt is finely ground with the addition of magnesium carbonate to make it pour easily. Ionized table salt has added iodine.

Sicilian Meatball Soup

Meatballs

2 eggs
1 lb. ground mix (beef, veal and pork)
Kosher salt and fresh cracked pepper to taste
1⁄4 cup grated Parmesan cheese
1 cup fresh bread crumbs
1⁄4 cup chopped Italian flat leaf parsley
1 cup vegetable oil for frying

Combine ingredients for meatballs. Roll into one inch balls and fry in hot oil. Drain and discard oil.

Soup

1 48-ounce can chicken broth
1 14-ounce can beef broth
1 cup sliced mushrooms
1 10-ounce box frozen chopped spinach, defrosted
1 40 1⁄2-ounce can white beans, rinsed and drained
2 cups marinara sauce
Dash hot sauce
1 lb. tiny pasta cooked al dente and drained

Combine all ingredients. Add fried meatballs and simmer for 30-40 minutes. Cover, stirring occasionally.

RIDING A HARLEY

There are certain advantages to being a passenger on a Harley Davidson. For one, you get to sightsee. Being on the back of a "cool" motorcycle is quite an experience. Clint and I certainly dress the part. Black leather chaps, jacket and gloves, sunglasses, and black cowboy boots complete our "biker" look.

The roar of the engine notifies other people that a "Harley" is nearby. Lots of people wave, especially the kids. They watch, their eyes following the bike as it goes by. Women glance longingly and I smile with delight.

Riding on any Harley can be great fun, but riding on Clint's bike is a blast! Clint keeps his motorcycle in the dining room. How is that for love? A Dyna-Wide Glide '93, with gorgeous black and red paint. Custom flames on the engine, chrome shining from every angle and the black leather studded saddlebags with matching handlebar bags accessorize the look. The front wheel with 80 spokes sparkles in the sunlight, blinding with shine as we thunder by.

A typical ride starts early in the morning, usually on a Sunday. After negotiating Interstate 95 (riding next to a semi-truck is a little scary) we turn off onto the side roads of Delaware and into Maryland. Now this is fun! As the passenger, you really get to enjoy the scenery, sights, sounds and smells. You get to think a lot when on the back of a bike...about nature, about life, and about where to eat lunch!

We stop for crab cakes and iced tea. I take off my helmet and take out my ear plugs. Wow, I can hear again! After lunch, a crowd gathers around Clint's bike. (I told you it was a looker!) I think Clint loves this part most of all.

The ride home seems shorter, although there is more traffic. I get to wave at more kids and look at the envy in other women's eyes. This is the part I love best. We return home. Clint washes his bike. I reluctantly take off my leathers 'til next time.

Autumn Pumpkin and Pear Soup

- 2 tablespoons butter, melted
- 2 tablespoons flour
- 2 tablespoons pear syrup
- 1 15-ounce can of pears, drained and chopped (reserve 2 tablespoons syrup)
- 8 cups chicken broth
- 2 29-ounce cans pumpkin (not pumpkin pie mix)
- 2 tablespoons honey
- Kosher salt and fresh cracked pepper to taste
- 1 cup light cream

Make roux by combining melted butter and flour over low heat until smooth and silky, 5-10 minutes. Add syrup and chicken broth. Whisk until smooth. Add pears and remaining ingredients. Simmer 20-25 minutes stirring occasionally.

To make a roux, use equal parts butter and flour. Melt the butter first and then add the flour. Cook over low heat stirring frequently with a wooden spoon until mixture is golden and satiny, at least 5-10 minutes. Add any liquid slowly, then whisk briskly to incorporate and avoid lumps.

Country Crab Chowder

One of my favorite recipes.

4-5 tablespoons butter
2-3 tablespoons olive oil
1 cup diced celery
1 1/2 cups chopped onion
1 cup diced carrots
1/4 cup chopped Italian flat leaf parsley
2 leeks, chopped
1/2 cup chopped scallions
2 cups diced and boiled red bliss potatoes
Kosher salt and fresh cracked pepper
1 teaspoon Old Bay seasoning
Dash hot sauce
1 29-ounce can plum tomatoes, cut up (or use chef cut tomatoes)
6 cups chicken broth
1-2 lbs. jumbo lump crabmeat

In butter and oil sauté celery, onion, carrot, parsley, leeks and scallion until fragrant, 10-15 minutes. Season with salt and pepper. Add potatoes. Add remaining ingredients and simmer 30-40 minutes.

When a recipe calls for plum tomatoes you can substitute marinara sauce for a wonderful flavor.

Pick A Peppercorn

- Black peppercorns are sun-dried green peppercorn berries, characterized by an aromatic, clean and pungent flavor.
- Green peppercorns are dried, unripe fruit of the pepper plant with a milder and fruitier flavor.
- White peppercorns have a milder flavor and are preferred over black for cooking because they do not darken delicate sauces.
- Pink peppercorns are not really peppercorns at all. They are mildly toxic in large quantities and their culinary value is primarily visual.

Herbed Tomato Soup with Goat Cheese Croutons

4 tablespoons butter, melted
2 cloves garlic, chopped
1 cup chopped onion
1 cup chopped celery
1/4 cup chopped chives
1/4 cup shredded basil
1 teaspoon honey
Kosher salt and fresh cracked pepper to taste
2 cups marinara sauce
1 48-ounce can chicken broth
1/2 cup light cream

Sauté garlic, onion and celery in butter until soft, 15-20 minutes. Add chives, basil, seasoning and honey. Cook until honey is dissolved. Add remaining ingredients and simmer 20-30 minutes. Garnish bowl of soup with croutons.

Goat Cheese Croutons

12 bread rounds
4 ounces cream cheese, softened
4 ounces goat cheese, softened

Combine goat cheese and cream cheese in food processor. Spread mixture on bread rounds. Toast uncovered at 350º for 15-20 minutes until golden. Croutons can be made ahead of time.

When making soups there are a variety of small pastas to choose from. Always cook pasta just before adding to soup. It's OK to cook al dente, which means firm to the bite. It will soften more in the soup. Use different kinds for a nice change—acini de pepe, pastine, ditalini, riso, orzo—just to name a few.

SWEET TEA

I am intrigued by Southerners, a group of Americans unique unto themselves. I can listen for hours to their charming southern drawl. Whenever I hear that singsong, soothing, melodious talk, I am transported to the wrap-around porch of a southern plantation, magnolia trees blooming in the distance, a glass of sweet iced tea on a silver tray. The aroma of honeysuckle floats in the air. Savannah, Charleston, Charlotte, Atlanta, there are plenty of cities and ample opportunity to experience this southern delight.

From the rolling hills of West Virginia to the dewy moss on the sycamore trees in Georgia, the South is rich in history and culture. From pit barbecue to fried chicken to creamy grits, the foods entice with mouth watering goodness. Hospitality grows in abundance in the South; the people are warm and friendly. The pace is gentle, slow enough to enjoy.

If the opportunity arises, visit this wonderful part of the country. You will return home sweetened and relaxed.

Mom's Wedding Bell Soup

There are several steps to making this soup but it's worthwhile because it is so delicious! Other versions are known as traditional Italian wedding soup.

Little Meatballs

- 2 eggs
- 1 lb. ground mix (beef, pork and veal)
- 1 cup fresh bread crumbs
- 1⁄4 cup grated Parmesan cheese
- Kosher salt and fresh cracked pepper
- 1⁄4 cup chopped Italian flat leaf parsley
- 1 cup vegetable oil for frying

Combine all ingredients. Roll into 1 inch or smaller meatballs. Fry in oil until brown. Drain and discard oil.

Frittata

- 3 eggs, well beaten
- 1⁄2 cup grated Parmesan cheese
- 1 tablespoon chopped Italian flat leaf parsley
- 1 tablespoon butter, melted

Beat together eggs, cheese and parsley. Cook in butter making a large omelet. Cool and cut into small pieces.

Soup

- 3 48-ounce cans chicken broth
- 2 packages frozen chopped spinach, defrost, rinse and squeeze dry
- 1 box acini de pepe pasta (tiny pearls of pasta), cooked al dente and drained

In large stock pot combine chicken broth, spinach, pasta, fried meatballs and cut-up frittata. Simmer uncovered 20-30 minutes. If soup gets thick the next day, just add more chicken broth.

A Sweet Mystery

We call sweet potatoes yams and vice-versa. Actually, the true yam is a tropical vegetable and what we think of as yams is a paler version of sweet potato. Sweet potatoes range from pale yellow to a rich dark orange. The darker the flesh the sweeter the potato.

Sweet Potato Soup with Buttered Crispy Pecans

2 sweet potatoes, peeled and cubed

1 baking potato, peeled and cubed

5 cups chicken broth (using 3 cups and then 2 cups)

4 tablespoons butter

1 1/2 cups chopped onion

1 cup chopped leeks

2 cloves garlic, chopped

1 cup chopped carrots

Kosher salt and fresh cracked pepper to taste

In 3 cups chicken broth cook potatoes until tender. Set aside to cool and DO NOT drain broth. Sauté onion, leeks, garlic and carrots in butter. Season with salt and pepper. Add remaining 2 cups of broth and cook until soft. To this add potato mixture and purée in small batches in a food processor. Simmer 20-25 minutes. Garnish bowl of soup with buttered pecans.

Buttered Crispy Pecans

1 cup chopped pecans

2 tablespoons butter, melted

Kosher salt to taste

Cook pecans in butter with salt until crispy, 10-15 minutes.

Leeks are very sandy, and unlike scallions, you need to discard the dark green tops and cut off root ends. To clean, cut leeks in half lengthwise and then cut up in half circles. Immerse in cold water swishing them around to dislodge any grit and sand. Rinse well.

Butternut Squash and Corn Chowder

3 lbs. butternut squash, peeled and cubed

3 cups chicken broth

2 tablespoons butter, melted

1 1/2 cups chopped onion

2 cloves garlic, minced

2 cups frozen corn, defrosted

Kosher salt and fresh cracked pepper to taste

Cook butternut squash in 3 cups of chicken broth 15-20 minutes or until tender. DO NOT DRAIN. Cool and purée in food processor in batches. In stock pot, sauté onion and garlic in butter until fragrant. Add puréed squash and corn. Season with salt and pepper. Simmer 30-35 minutes.

Chilled Red Raspberry Soup

1 16-ounce bag frozen raspberries, defrosted

1 cup apple juice

1/4 cup honey

1/2 cup light cream

Fresh raspberries for garnish

Heat apple juice and honey until dissolved, 5-10 minutes. Combine with defrosted raspberries in food processor until puréed. Add light cream and chill. Garnish bowl of soup with fresh raspberries.

Tomato and Bread Soup

4-6 tablespoons olive oil

2 tablespoons butter

2 stalks celery, chopped

2 cloves garlic, minced

1 1/2 cups chopped onion

Kosher salt and fresh cracked pepper to taste

4 cups chicken broth

4 cups chef cut tomatoes

10 fresh basil leaves, shredded

6 slices day-old Italian bread* torn into pieces (about 2 cups)

1/2 cup grated Parmesan cheese

Sauté celery, garlic and onion in oil and butter. Season and cook until transparent, 15-20 minutes. Add broth and tomatoes. Cook additional 15 minutes. Before serving add bread pieces, fresh basil and grated cheese. Garnish bowl of soup with drizzle of olive oil and more cheese.

**Make sure the bread you use is a coarse, dense Italian bread. (Stale is best.) DO NOT USE SOFT ROLLS.*

Chef cut tomatoes are plum tomatoes that have been coarsely chopped. Use the liquid too—DO NOT DRAIN THAT GOOD STUFF!

Summertime Strawberry Soup

1 quart fresh sweet strawberries, cut up

3 tablespoons honey

1 cup vanilla yogurt

1/2 cup white wine

1/2 cup sour cream

Dash allspice

Combine in food processor until smooth. Serve chilled. Serve this soup in a demitasse or espresso cup with a strawberry garnish on the saucer.

Club Orient Gazpacho

This was my lunch every day during a trip to St. Martin; eaten, of course, with a baguette and butter!

3 slices white bread

4-5 cloves garlic

3 tablespoons lemon juice

10 ripe plum tomatoes

5 scallions

3 cucumbers, peeled and seeded

1 green pepper, seeded

1 red pepper, seeded

1 yellow pepper, seeded

1 46-ounce can tomato juice

3 tablespoons balsamic vinegar

5 tablespoons olive oil

Kosher salt and fresh cracked pepper to taste

Combine first three ingredients in food processor and set aside. Coarsely chop vegetables. Purée in food processor in batches. Add to bread mixture. Add juice, vinegar, olive oil, salt and pepper. Chill and serve.

Using a vegetable peeler, take the outer dark green skin off a cucumber. Cut in half. Take a regular kitchen teaspoon and run it down the center to scrape all the seeds out. Now it's ready to dice!

Making Lists

People often ask me how I accomplish so much. When cooking and preparing for a party for themselves, they call me and tell me I must be crazy to be in this business. Well, no doubt about it...catering is very hard work! Many times when the "in season" strikes, I am catering multiple parties in just one weekend. Each party is unique with its own personality and pulse and each demands special attention to make it perfect.

One thing I have found that helps me keep everything straight is to make a daily list of the things I would like to do in a day. On the list are things as simple as making my calls or remembering to mail something, along with items needed to be cooked or defrosted or sorted. Not only does this keep me on track, there is nothing better than crossing items off the list that have been accomplished. It is mini goal-setting and my reward is completion.

Try making a daily list. You'll be amazed at how much more you can accomplish in just one day. Remember that nothing is too small or insignificant for the list. And the best part—crossing out! I like to make my list at night for the next day. It gets my mind and body ready for the day ahead and allows me to 'let go' of agendas and tasks so I rest peacefully.

Set mini goals, make a list and see how much more you can do with less stress. Remember that the best part is feeling organized and accomplishing goals!

The Power of Positive Thinking

I have a little yellowed newspaper clipping taped to my desk, it says; If you think you can, you will. If you think you can't, you won't. My father always said to me, "If you don't try, you've already lost, but if you do try, there is a chance you will win." A chance is better than none. Start to change your thoughts. Think positive, look at life as good, rain as beautiful, Monday as exciting. Why lose a day a week by hating Mondays? Life is short and goes by very fast. Enjoy every second; your life will be full. When you are happy and fulfilled, those around you share your rewards.

SALADS AND DRESSINGS

SALAD HINTS >> *I have a lot of recipes for fabulous salads. There is no better way to entertain than with room temperature food. This allows the hostess to enjoy the party. Salads are always best made the day they are served, but there are a few tricks to the trade. I do as much prep work as possible and make the dressings a few days ahead. Be sure to label them before refrigerating so it's not a guessing game when you need to toss things together.*

I will cook the pasta or potatoes, blanch the veggies, do all of my chopping, etc., in advance but keep all the ingredients separate until the morning of the party. Then I can just toss everything together, put it all in my fancy pottery and store in the refrigerator until party time. Fresh tasting and beautiful salads every time and the cook and hostess look great, too!

Olive Oil: Regional Differences

- Spanish oils are golden and buttery
- Italian oils are peppery and delicate
- Greek oils are robust
- California oils are smooth and clean tasting

Grading Olive Oils

- Extra Virgin—considered finest and fruitiest. The deeper the color, the more intense the olive flavor.
- Virgin—higher level of acidity
- Fino—blend of extra virgin and virgin
- Light—lighter in color and fragrance and has little of the classic olive oil flavor

Tomato and Feta Salad

1 lb. feta cheese, crumbled

6 scallions, chopped

1 tablespoon chopped Italian flat leaf parsley

12-15 plum tomatoes, sliced

1 thinly sliced red onion

Dressing

1 cup olive oil

1 teaspoon lime juice

1 teaspoon dried oregano

1 teaspoon dried dill

Kosher salt and fresh cracked pepper to taste

Layer tomatoes, red onion, scallion and parsley on a platter. Sprinkle with feta cheese. Combine dressing and pour over tomatoes.

Green Bean Almondine Salad

3 lbs. green beans, cooked until tender

3⁄4 cup olive oil

3-4 cloves garlic, minced

2 tablespoons chopped Italian flat leaf parsley

Kosher salt and fresh cracked pepper to taste

1 cup sliced almonds, toasted

Sauté garlic in hot oil until fragrant. Add parsley and season with salt and pepper. Toss with green beans and almonds. Serve at room temperature.

To blanch green beans, bring water to a boil. Add trimmed green beans and let water return to a boil. DO NOT COVER or beans will turn gray. Cook until crisp and bright green. It will take about 5-7 minutes. If you are unsure if beans are cooked just taste one!

To toast nuts, layer nuts on cookie sheet and bake at 350º for 10-15 minutes, stirring occasionally. Nuts have a high oil content and will burn easily—if you smell them, check them. You can toast nuts ahead and then freeze them. I like to use sliced almonds with the skin on for a nice looking salad.

Pasta Salad with Sun-Dried Tomatoes and Asparagus

- 1 lb. penne pasta, cooked, drained and sprinkled with kosher salt and 2 tablespoons olive oil
- 6 tablespoons olive oil
- 2-3 cloves garlic, minced
- 1 tablespoon minced Italian flat leaf parsley
- 1 cup chopped sun-dried tomatoes
- 1/2 cup marinara sauce
- Kosher salt and fresh cracked pepper
- 1 lb. asparagus, cut on an angle and cooked until tender
- 1/2 cup grated Parmesan cheese

Sauté garlic, parsley and sun-dried tomatoes in hot oil until fragrant. Add marinara sauce and toss with asparagus and pasta. Sprinkle with cheese. Serve at room temperature for a delicious meal.

When trimming asparagus bend the stalk. Where it breaks is generally the tough end, about 1-2 inches from the bottom. Trim the rest of the stalk with a knife.

TIME FOR DINNER

Everyone's idea of dinnertime is different, geared toward their lifestyle and customs. We always ate early growing up. I think my mom thought that the earlier she fed us, the earlier she could get us to bed.

Now it's a different story. We eat dinner at 7, 8 or 9 p.m., depending on our day and where we are. Most people in European countries eat very late. Most restaurants in Italy don't open before 7 p.m., and no one will show up until 8. In Spain and Portugal, 10-11 p.m. is the norm for the evening meal. The feast goes on for hours, two or three at least, sometimes lingering all night long. No wonder most Europeans eat a light breakfast of coffee and bread. Our lives and our eating habits adjust to our environment.

If I'm adding a vegetable—such as asparagus or broccoli—to pasta, I rinse it, cut it up and toss it into the boiling water with the pasta just before it is done cooking. This way I have my pasta and vegetable done at the same time with just one pot to clean!

Cajun Cole Slaw

- 1 16-ounce bag cole slaw mix
- 1 10-ounce bag shredded red cabbage
- 1 10-ounce bag shredded carrots
- 1 red pepper, seeded and diced
- 1/4 cup chopped Italian flat leaf parsley

Dressing

- 1 cup mayonnaise
- 1 tablespoon red wine vinegar
- Dash hot sauce
- Kosher salt and fresh cracked pepper to taste
- 2 teaspoons celery seeds
- 1 tablespoon sugar
- 1 tablespoon Cajun seasoning

Whisk all ingredients for a smooth dressing. Mix together cole slaw, cabbage, carrots, pepper and parsley. Fold in dressing.

You can prepare dressing one day ahead but this recipe is best when tossed together when ready to eat. It's colorful and deliciously different.

I love the preshredded bags of cole slaw, carrots and cabbage. They make life easier when I want to cook but am too busy. Use any short cuts you can!

Spicy Shrimp Salad

1⁄2 cup olive oil
1 tablespoon chopped garlic
2 tablespoons chopped Italian flat leaf parsley
1 tablespoon hot sauce
1 teaspoon seafood seasoning
1 teaspoon lemon juice
3 lbs. frozen cooked and cleaned shrimp, defrosted and drained well
1 cup diced red onion
1 cup chopped celery
1 red pepper, diced
1 yellow pepper, diced

Sauté garlic, parsley, hot sauce and seafood seasoning in hot oil for 5-10 minutes or until fragrant. Add lemon juice. Combine shrimp with onion, celery and pepper. Toss with olive oil dressing.

Caesar Tortellini Salad Primavera

4-6 tablespoons garlic
2 tablespoons Dijon mustard
2 tablespoons honey
1⁄4 cup red wine vinegar
1 teaspoon Worcestershire sauce
1⁄2 cup grated Parmesan cheese
Kosher salt and fresh cracked pepper to taste
1 cup olive oil
2 lbs. tri-colored cooked cheese tortellini
2 cups of your favorite freshly cut vegetables; try carrots, zucchini, grape tomatoes and yellow squash

Combine the first seven ingredients in a food processor. With processor running, slowly add oil. The dressing will be thick and creamy. Toss dressing with tortellini and vegetables and serve.

Dressing can be prepared a few days ahead and refrigerated. This is a great dressing for salads as well as raw vegetables.

Broccoli Salad and Balsamic Dressing

4 cups chopped fresh broccoli
1 red onion, chopped fine
2 tablespoons capers
1 cup olive oil
2 tablespoons balsamic vinegar
2 tablespoons honey
Kosher salt and fresh cracked pepper

Mix together olive oil, vinegar, honey, salt and pepper until thick. Combine broccoli, onion and capers. Toss broccoli mixture with dressing. Serve cold.

Capers are the bud of a plant grown in the Mediterranean. Some hedges can grow up to 10 feet high! They come in different sizes from tiny pearls to caper berries with a long stem. Capers come packed in a briny liquid or salt and should be rinsed before using. You can usually find them in your local supermarket's olive section.

When cutting up broccoli be sure to use part of the stem. Peel the outer layers with a small paring knife and cut up into chunks. It is flavorful and delicious.

Greek Salad

3 cucumbers peeled, seeded and diced
1 red onion, chopped
6 plum tomatoes, chopped
1⁄2 cup crumbled feta cheese
1⁄2 cup imported black olives

Dressing

6 tablespoons olive oil
2 tablespoons red wine vinegar
1 tablespoon lemon juice
1 teaspoon dried oregano
Kosher salt and fresh cracked pepper to taste

Toss all vegetables together and mix with salad dressing. A very filling salad!

Dijon Honey Red Bliss Potato Salad

I love to use baby red bliss potatoes for potato salad. The skin is tender and colorful so you don't have to peel them. They are not starchy so they won't absorb a lot of dressing.

Dressing

1 cup mayonnaise
2 tablespoons honey
2 tablespoons Dijon mustard
Dash hot sauce
Kosher salt and fresh cracked pepper to taste
3 lbs. red bliss potatoes, cut up and cooked
1/2 cup cut up celery
1/2 cup cut up scallion
1 red pepper, seeded and diced
1/2 cup chopped Italian flat leaf parsley

Whisk first 4 ingredients together until smooth. Add salt and pepper to taste. Combine remaining ingredients in separate bowl and toss with dressing.

To cook potatoes perfectly, cut up and drop into cold, unsalted water. (Salt will cause potatoes to break up.) Bring water to a boil and cook 5-7 minutes. (The small pieces will cook quickly.) Drain and rinse well. Salt potatoes while they are still hot, tasting as you go. (Potatoes may take more salt then you think they need.) Mix with remaining ingredients or refrigerate and mix just prior to serving.

Caribbean Jerk Rice Salad

This salad goes a long way. Use it for a big crowd!

1 red onion, chopped
1 red pepper, chopped
1 yellow pepper, chopped
1/2 cup chopped scallion
1 cup black beans, cooked
1 cup frozen corn, defrosted
1/4 cup chopped Italian flat leaf parsley
3 cups cooked white rice

Combine these ingredients and toss with dressing.

Dressing

1 cup olive oil
2 cloves garlic
1 tablespoon chopped ginger
1 teaspoon hot sauce
1 tablespoon lime juice
1/2 teaspoon cumin
1/2 teaspoon crushed red pepper
1/2 teaspoon allspice
Kosher salt and fresh cracked pepper to taste

Sauté garlic and ginger in hot oil until soft. Add remaining ingredients and toss with rice mixture.

Maybe it's the Italian in me, but I hate to cook rice! When a recipe calls for it, I often visit my local Chinese restaurant for plain, steamed, white rice. (And they always throw in some fortune cookies for my dessert!)

"Corny" Corn Salad

4 cups frozen corn, defrosted and drained
1 cup cooked black beans
1 large red onion, diced
1 green pepper, seeded and diced
1 red pepper, seeded and diced
2 stalks celery, chopped
1/2 cup chopped scallion

Dressing

1/4 cup sugar
1/2 cup olive oil
1/4 cup vinegar
1 tablespoon lime juice
Kosher salt and fresh cracked pepper to taste

Whisk together ingredients for dressing. Combine salad ingredients and toss with dressing.

You can cook beans from scratch, or use canned beans as a great substitution. They come in a milky liquid and should be drained and rinsed well.

Tuscan Bean and Tuna Salad

The oil in the tuna fish becomes the dressing for this salad.

3 6-ounce cans Italian tuna fish (do not drain)
1 40-ounce can white beans, rinsed and drained
1 cup chopped red onion
2 stalks celery, chopped
1 tablespoon chopped Italian flat leaf parsley
Kosher salt and fresh cracked pepper

Combine all ingredients.

You can buy Italian tuna fish in almost any supermarket. It is packed in olive oil and is very delicious! You can substitute any tuna packed in oil. Be sure not to drain that wonderful flavor.

Sensational Shrimp and Asparagus Salad

1/2 cup ketchup
1/4 cup olive oil
1 tablespoon lemon juice
3/4 cup mayonnaise
1 teaspoon Dijon mustard
1 teaspoon Worcestershire sauce
Dash hot sauce
Dash paprika
1 teaspoon horseradish
Kosher salt and fresh cracked pepper
3 lbs. frozen cooked and cleaned shrimp, defrosted and drained well
2 lbs. asparagus

Whisk together all ingredients, except shrimp and asparagus, until smooth. Cut asparagus on an angle. Drop into boiling water and cook until tender but still bright green. Toss with shrimp and dressing. Can be served over a bed of lettuce.

Sicilian Orange Salad

6 navel or blood oranges, peeled and sliced
1 cup thinly sliced red onion
1/2 cup imported black olives
1/2 cup crumbled ricotta salata or feta cheese
1/2 cup olive oil
1 tablespoon red wine vinegar
Kosher salt and fresh cracked pepper

On a platter layer sliced oranges, top with onion, sprinkle with olives and cheese. Combine the oil and vinegar and drizzle all over. Season with salt and pepper.

Blood oranges are juicy and very tasty. You can sometimes find them in your local gourmet produce markets. Navel oranges will work well with this recipe.

Ricotta salata cheese is a dry, crumbly and very tasty type of ricotta cheese. It is available at gourmet cheese shops or Italian markets. Feta cheese makes a great substitution.

Pacific Rim Orzo Salad

1 lb. orzo pasta (looks like rice)
2 tablespoons olive oil
4 stalks celery, chopped
4 carrots, shredded
3 scallions, chopped
1 red pepper, diced
1 cup golden raisins

Dressing

1/2 cup olive oil
1 tablespoon sesame oil
3 tablespoons soy sauce
1 teaspoon lemon juice
1 tablespoon honey
1/2 teaspoon red pepper flakes
1 teaspoon chopped ginger
1 teaspoon chopped garlic
2 tablespoons toasted sesame seeds.

Cook pasta al dente. Drain and toss with oil. Mix with remaining salad ingredients. Combine all dressing ingredients and toss with pasta mixture.

Italian Bread Salad

This Tuscan peasant salad is deliciously different.

1 cup olive oil
1/4 cup balsamic vinegar
Kosher salt and fresh cracked pepper
6 plum tomatoes, cut up
2 cucumbers, peeled, seeded and diced
1 red pepper, cut into thin strips
1 red onion, chopped
1 cup imported black olives
1 tablespoon capers
1/2 cup shredded fresh basil
5 cups coarsely chopped day-old Italian bread

Combine oil and vinegar. Season with salt and pepper. Toss with remaining ingredients. Let sit 20 minutes before serving.

ON THE ROAD AGAIN

Clint was on a mission; we were planning a road trip and taking his truck. The polishing cloth and can of wax were ready and waiting. A new cooler in the back, window cleaner, paper towels for any wayward bird dropping and his new acquisition—a CB radio! We were all set to go, privy to trucker's conversation and any lurking state troopers.

Traveling south, we could hear the drawl in the truckers' voices on the CB, "C'mon C'mon, bear in the right." Not only were we warned of state troopers with radar, but we also received weather reports, traffic reports, accounts of local foods, descriptions of other drivers and just normal chitchat. Conversations were respectful and always courteous. It made our eight-hour trip a very entertaining one.

We were on the road, traveling to Bristol, Tennessee, on one of our trips to a NASCAR Race. I love NASCAR! A different city hosts the NASCAR race each week. We've made it a goal to visit as many of these places as possible. Following NASCAR races each week has broadened my horizons to our big, beautiful country. This is great fun. We get to see the countryside, visit historical landmarks, taste local foods and talk to wonderful and friendly people from different states. Along the way, we also stop to visit local Harley Davidson dealers to get a t-shirt. Our collection is growing with varied and colorful styles.

Different interests can bring great pleasure and wonderful experiences. We keep an open mind and a fun attitude when we travel. Stopping when we want to, our agenda is loose. This way, all impromptu moments are special, too! Take a road trip across this beautiful country. There's a lot to see. And don't forget your CB! C'mon C'mon!

I serve this salad in a hollowed-out loaf of round Italian bread. I use the scooped out center for the bread in this recipe.

Basically Balsamic

Traditionally, true balsamic vinegar is made by boiling the juice of white grapes into a concentrate and then pouring it into wooden barrels to age slowly.

- Add a few drops to a spinach salad, dressing or fruit salad.
- Stir into pan juices of roast veal, beef or pork.
- Add it to a tomato sauce for depth of flavor.
- Sprinkle over strawberries.

Red Bliss Potatoes with Tomato Bacon Dressing

5 lbs. red bliss potatoes, cut up and cooked
6 plum tomatoes, chopped
1/4 cup chopped Italian flat leaf parsley
1 lb. bacon, cut up and cooked (drain and reserve 1/4 cup bacon drippings)

Dressing

1/2 cup olive oil
1/4 cup bacon drippings
1/4 cup balsamic vinegar
1 tablespoon brown sugar
Kosher salt and fresh cracked pepper
1 teaspoon Dijon mustard

Whisk dressing ingredients until combined. Set aside. Toss together potatoes, tomatoes, parsley and bacon along with dressing.

Three Bean and Artichoke Salad

1 1/2 lbs. green beans, trimmed and cooked until tender
15-ounce can butter beans, drained and rinsed
15-ounce can red kidney beans, drained and rinsed
1 cup chopped artichoke hearts
1/2 cup chopped roasted red peppers
2 tablespoons chopped Italian flat leaf parsley

Dressing

1/2 cup olive oil
1 tablespoon coarse grain mustard
1 teaspoon sugar
1 tablespoon lemon juice
2 cloves garlic, minced
Kosher salt and fresh cracked pepper to taste

Combine dressing ingredients and mix until smooth. Toss salad ingredients with dressing.

I prefer to use unseasoned canned artichokes to the ones in olive oil and spices. They have a fresher flavor. Just rinse and drain well. You can also use frozen artichoke hearts.

Orange Slices with Honey and Almonds

I use this as a light dessert, too!

6 navel oranges, peeled and sliced thin
1/2 cup honey
1/4 cup triple sec
Pinch cinnamon
1/2 cup toasted sliced almonds

In saucepan, warm honey with triple sec and cinnamon until honey melts and is combined with liquor. Drizzle mixture over a platter of sliced oranges. Sprinkle with almonds.

Triple sec is an orange liqueur. You can substitute plain orange juice.

Lemony Asparagus and New Potato Salad

1 1⁄2 lbs. asparagus, cut up and cooked
20 baby bliss potatoes, cut up and cooked
4-6 tablespoons olive oil
1 teaspoon lemon juice
Lemon zest from one lemon
Kosher salt and fresh cracked pepper
1 tablespoon chopped fresh dill

Mix potatoes with asparagus. Whisk remaining ingredients together and toss with potato mixture. Garnish with fresh lemon slices and dill.

Asparagus can be sandy. To clean well, cut a half inch off bottom of stalk and submerge in cold water for a few minutes. This forces the head of the asparagus to open and release any grit or sand. Rinse well.

Specialty oils can be found in the gourmet section of your supermarket. They do not have a long shelf life so store them in the refrigerator. The oil will get cloudy in the refrigerator but clear when you bring it to room temperature.

Tarragon Chicken Salad

These make delicious little sandwiches served on mini croissants.

4 whole boneless chicken breasts, cooked and cut into cubes
1⁄2–3⁄4 cup mayonnaise
1 teaspoon Dijon mustard
Kosher salt and fresh cracked pepper to taste
1 tablespoon fresh, or 1 teaspoon dried tarragon
2 stalks celery, cut up
Optional: 1⁄2 cup chopped walnuts
1⁄2 cup sliced grapes

Mix the mayonnaise with the mustard. Combine with remaining ingredients and chill.

To cook chicken for chicken salad, spray a baking sheet with cooking spray and layer the chicken breast side by side, not too close. Bake at 350º for 20-25 minutes or until juices run clear. Allow to cool before cutting into cubes for the salad.

Tossed Salad with Hazelnut Dressing, Blue Cheese and Dried Cranberries

4-6 cups mixed greens
1 red onion, sliced thin
1⁄4 cup dried cranberries
1⁄4 cup toasted hazelnuts
1⁄4 cup blue cheese crumbles

Dressing

3⁄4 cup olive oil
1⁄4 cup hazelnut oil
1⁄4 cup white wine vinegar
2 tablespoon Dijon mustard
2 tablespoon honey
Kosher salt and fresh cracked pepper to taste

Combine dressing ingredients in food processor, adding oils last. Dressing can be prepared up to one week in advance.

Apple Spinach Salad

6 cups baby spinach leaves
2 Granny Smith apples, sliced
1/2 cup chopped walnuts, toasted
1/4 cup white raisins

Dressing

1 cup olive oil
1/4 cup apple cider vinegar
2 tablespoons honey
1/2 teaspoon celery seeds
1 clove garlic, minced
Kosher salt and fresh cracked pepper

Combine ingredients in food processor, adding oil last. Dressing can be prepared up to one week in advance. Layer baby spinach leaves, sprinkle apples, walnuts and raisins on top. Drizzle with dressing.

When cooking with apples, it is not necessary to peel them. The skins are good for you and they add color to your dish!

Colorful Christmas Salad with Cranberry Vinaigrette

6 cups red tipped lettuce
1 11-ounce can mandarin oranges, drained
1/2 cup sweetened dried cranberries
1/2 cup sliced red onion

Vinaigrette

1 cup olive oil
1/4 cup red wine vinegar
1/4 cup cranberry juice
1 tablespoon Dijon mustard
1 tablespoon honey
Kosher salt and fresh cracked pepper to taste

Combine all dressing ingredients in a food processor, adding oil last. Dressing can be prepared up to one week in advance. Layer lettuce, oranges and onion. Sprinkle with cranberries. Drizzle with vinaigrette.

Winter Spring Salad

When visiting southern Oregon a few years ago, we stayed at the Winter Spring Ranch, a breathtaking place! Lidia, the owner, made this salad for us when we arrived by motorcycle, wet and soggy from the rain!

6 cups mixed greens
2 clementines, peeled and sliced
1/2 cup shaved Parmesan cheese

Dressing

3 cloves garlic, minced
2 tablespoons Dijon mustard
2 tablespoons water
1 tablespoon honey
1/4 cup orange juice
1/4 cup balsamic vinegar
1 teaspoon curry powder
Kosher salt and fresh cracked pepper
1 cup olive oil

Curried Almonds

1/4 cup butter, melted
1/4 cup brown sugar
Dash curry powder
Kosher salt to taste
1 cup sliced almonds

Combine all dressing ingredients in food processor, adding oil last. Toss with salad. Mix together curried almonds and sprinkle over salad.

When chopping vegetables for a salad try to keep the size uniform. It's easier to eat and looks better, too.

Salad with Grilled Chicken in a Raspberry Honey Dijon Dressing with Parmesan Croutons

3 boneless chicken breasts cooked at 350º for 20-25 minutes, or until juices run clear. Grill on one side and slice.

Parmesan Croutons

1⁄2 stick butter, melted

4 tablespoons grated Parmesan cheese

1 clove garlic, chopped

2 cups Italian bread cut into cubes

Toss all ingredients together. Bake at 350º for 15-20 minutes, stirring occasionally.

Raspberry Honey-Dijon Dressing

1 cup olive oil

1⁄4 cup red wine vinegar

1 tablespoon honey

2 tablespoons Dijon mustard

1 tablespoon raspberry preserves

Kosher salt and fresh cracked pepper to taste

Dash of Worcestershire sauce

Combine dressing ingredients in food processor, adding oil last. Dressing can be prepared up to one week in advance.

Be My Honey

- Honey never spoils, so don't refrigerate.
- Honey has a tendency to granulate—restore to liquid by placing jar in a pan of warm water.
- Store honey in plastic squeeze bottles for easier handling and measuring.

Versatile Vinegar

- Removes price tags from glass, wood or china.
- White vinegar eliminates onion odors from hands.
- To remove stains from coffee cups, rub with salt and vinegar.
- Saucers of vinegar placed around the room will eliminate unpleasant cooking odors.
- A paste of salt and vinegar is a good copper cleaner.

Mixed Greens with Honey-Dijon Vinaigrette and Sugared Nuts

8-10 cups spring mix or mixed greens

Honey Dijon Vinaigrette

2-3 cloves garlic, minced

1 tablespoon honey

2 tablespoons Dijon mustard

1⁄2 cup grated Parmesan cheese

1⁄4 cup red wine vinegar

1 teaspoon Worcestershire sauce

Kosher salt and fresh cracked pepper to taste

1 cup olive oil

Sugared Nuts

8 tablespoons butter, melted

1 1⁄2 cups brown sugar

2 cups chopped pecans (you can substitute any kind of nut)

Combine all dressing ingredients in food processor, adding oil last, until thick and creamy. Dressing can be prepared up to one week in advance. Pour dressing over greens and top with sugared nuts.

To make sugared nuts, add sugar to melted butter until absorbed. Toss with chopped nuts and mix well. Refrigerate until ready to use, up to one week.

Mixed Green Salad with Strawberries and Balsamic Vinaigrette

6 cups mixed greens
1⁄2 cup chopped celery
1 cup fresh sliced strawberries
1⁄2 cup toasted pine nuts

Dressing

1 cup olive oil
1⁄4 cup balsamic vinegar
1 teaspoon sugar
Kosher salt and fresh cracked pepper to taste

Combine dressing ingredients. Toss greens with celery and strawberries, sprinkle with nuts and drizzle with dressing.

Cut up and toss summer sweet strawberries with a little bit of balsamic vinegar and fresh cracked pepper. A real treat and so delicious.

B.L.T. Salad

8 slices bacon, cut up and cooked until crisp
2 tomatoes, chopped
2 hard boiled eggs, chopped
6 cups chopped iceberg lettuce
1/2 cup slivered almonds, toasted

Honey Mustard Vinaigrette

1/4 cup vinegar
2 tablespoons Dijon mustard
1 tablespoon lemon juice
2 tablespoons honey
1 shallot, chopped
Kosher salt and fresh cracked pepper to taste
1 cup olive oil

Toss together salad ingredients. Combine all dressing ingredients in food processor, adding the oil last. Dress salad.

Older, rather than fresh eggs, work best for hard boiled eggs; they peel easier.

Caesar Salad with Spicy Shrimp and Homemade Croutons

6 cups romaine lettuce, torn

Dressing

2 cloves garlic
1⁄2 cup grated Parmesan cheese
1 tablespoon Dijon mustard
1 anchovy
1 tablespoon Worcestershire sauce
1 cup olive oil
1⁄4 cup red wine vinegar

Spicy Shrimp

1-2 lbs. frozen cooked and cleaned shrimp, defrosted and drained well
2 cloves garlic, chopped
1 tablespoon Old Bay seasoning
Dash hot sauce
2 tablespoons olive oil

Homemade Croutons

1⁄2 stick butter, melted
4 tablespoons grated Parmesan cheese
1 clove garlic, chopped
2 cups cubed Italian bread

Toss all crouton ingredients together and bake at 350º for 15-20 minutes until golden, stir occasionally.

Combine all dressing ingredients in food processor, adding oil last. Sauté garlic in hot oil. Add shrimp, seasoning and hot sauce. Toss together lettuce, croutons, shrimp and dressing.

A lot of people shy away from anchovies, but when used in a recipe cooked or cut up fine, the flavor is subtly enhanced.

Salad Dressings

Be creative and use these dressings on your favorite salads. Once you start to make your own salad dressings you will never go back to bottled again!

Orange Poppy Dressing

1/4 cup red wine vinegar
2 tablespoons honey
1 tablespoon Dijon mustard
1 teaspoon Worcestershire sauce
1 clove garlic, minced
1 shallot, chopped
1 tablespoon orange juice
Kosher salt and fresh cracked pepper to taste
1 tablespoon poppy seeds
1 cup olive oil

Combine all ingredients in food processor, adding oil last. Can be prepared up to one week ahead.

Spicy Ginger-Lime Dressing

This makes a wonderful salad with smoked salmon and capers over greens.

1 cup olive oil
1/4 cup rice wine vinegar
1 tablespoon lime juice
1 tablespoon brown sugar
1 teaspoon minced ginger
2 cloves garlic, minced
1/2 teaspoon hot sauce
Kosher salt and fresh cracked pepper to taste

Combine all ingredients in food processor, adding oil last. Can be prepared up to one week ahead.

If my salad dressing calls for fresh garlic and ginger, I sometimes like to soften the flavors by cooking them for a few minutes in olive oil and then adding the remaining ingredients. This adds a subtle flavor of garlic and ginger.

Dante's Dressing

2 cloves garlic, chopped
1/2 cup grated Parmesan cheese
1 cup olive oil
1/4 cup red wine vinegar
2 tablespoons ketchup
1 teaspoon horseradish
Kosher salt and fresh cracked pepper

Combine all ingredients in food processor, adding oil last. Can be prepared up to one week ahead.

Cosmo Cranberry Vinaigrette

Great when garnished with dried, sweetened cranberries!

1 cup olive oil
1 tablespoon red wine vinegar
2 tablespoons lime juice
1 teaspoon vodka
1/4 cup cranberry juice
1 tablespoon honey
Kosher salt and fresh cracked pepper to taste

Combine all ingredients in food processor, adding oil last. Can be prepared up to one week ahead.

Maple Balsamic Dressing

1 cup olive oil
1/4 cup balsamic vinaigrette
3 tablespoons maple syrup
2 teaspoons Dijon mustard
1 clove garlic, minced
Kosher salt and fresh cracked pepper to taste

Combine all ingredients in food processor, adding oil last. Can be prepared up to one week ahead.

Dolci Bisogna "Sweet Dreams"

Some people consider daydreaming a waste of time. I remember my teachers in school saying, "Stop daydreaming. Your head is in the clouds." Now I know differently. Daydreaming brings dreams closer to reality. The things we think about, we make real. Everything that is in our life right now was a thought, a wish, a dream at one time. A little daydreaming is good. Go ahead and remember to wish for the stars!

LOVE IS AN INGREDIENT

It's important to compliment the cook no matter what you think of the meal. Since time, effort and love go into preparing a meal, and no one sets out to serve a bad meal, the cook deserves your compliments.

First Things First

As women we always take care of others. We tend to our families, friends, houses and gardens. We run around in a busy life trying to make everything go right and everyone happy. More often we put ourselves last. We're tired, stressed and overworked! How can we smile? We run around like a chicken without a head (my mother's expression). I think we need to take care of first things first—ourselves! During especially crazy holiday times, when baking, cooking and organizing seem endless. STOP and take a few minutes for yourself. Go to your room, leaf through a magazine. I have piles beside my bed that are waiting to be read. Close your eyes, go to a far off place and daydream. Your thoughts are real, what starts in your mind can be in your life. Give yourself some daydream time. You'll feel happy and less stressed. Be good to yourself first! Then you can take care of business.

MAIN ENTRÉES

NIGHT TALKS

With just stars and a few candles to illuminate the night, Clint and I lay in bed to talk and talk and talk. About places we have been, food we have eaten, people we have met and dreams we have for the future. About growing up, our families and our goals. Every night a different discussion. Together for twenty years, we still haven't run out of conversation!

Memories of our childhoods are dredged up. We laugh about things we did and dreamed when we were five or ten years old. We talk about our family tree and our children. We relive our vacations, sometimes minute by minute...where we had coffee or a pastry (our favorite thing to do!), where we got lost (almost every trip), how much we buy (I buy and he carries). These talks help us to relive, rethink and reshape our lives. It's a very important time when we question or confirm or just reminisce. We go to bed laughing, smiling and loving each other a bit more each night.

Communication is the most important part of a relationship; without it you are strangers in the same home, with it you always know that everything will be OK no matter what! Keep your conversations going. It's living and enjoying your life's precious moments.

Beef Brisket with Fall Vegetables

4-5 lb. beef brisket
Kosher salt and fresh cracked pepper to taste
4 carrots, chopped coarsely
4 potatoes, cut up
4 celery stalks, chopped coarsely
2 large onions, chopped
3 cloves garlic
1 package onion soup mix
1 cup water
1/2 cup red wine
1 cup chicken or beef broth
1 cup ketchup

Season brisket with salt and pepper. Put in a Dutch oven and cover with vegetables. In saucepan, combine onion soup mix, water, wine, broth and ketchup. Bring to a boil and then pour over brisket. Cover and cook at 350º for 2 1/2 hours.

Best Beef Barbecue

3-4 lb. London Broil
1/2 cup Worcestershire sauce
1/4 cup red wine vinegar
1 tablespoon hot pepper sauce
4 cups ketchup
1/4 cup brown sugar
1 tablespoon paprika
1 tablespoon soy sauce
Kosher salt and fresh cracked pepper to taste
1 teaspoon celery seed

Place London broil in Dutch oven. Combine remaining ingredients in saucepan and cook 10-15 minutes. Pour half of the sauce over meat. Cover and cook at 350º for 2-21/2 hours. Let cool. Remove meat from sauce and shred. Add the remaining sauce.

Prime Rib Roast with Horseradish Sauce and Spicy Bourbon Sauce

1 14-15 lb. Prime Rib roast, tied
(serves 10-12 people)

Rare 130º // Medium 140º // Well Done 160º

Dry Rub

1 teaspoon salt

1 teaspoon pepper

1 teaspoon granulated garlic

1⁄2 teaspoon paprika

Combine ingredients and rub on roast 1 hour prior to cooking. Roast uncovered at 350º until desired temperature is reached internally.

Horseradish Sauce

1 cup mayonnaise

2 tablespoons horseradish

2 tablespoons mustard

Combine ingredients and serve with roast.

Spicy Bourbon Sauce

3 tablespoons butter, melted

1⁄4 cup brown sugar

1⁄4 cup bourbon

1⁄2 cup coarse mustard

1 teaspoon hot sauce

2 tablespoons mayonnaise

Melt butter and whisk together with remaining ingredients. Serve hot or cold.

When roasting meats a cooking thermometer is a must. There is no guess work and you will never over or under cook your meat again.

Let your cooked meat "rest" for 10-20 minutes before slicing. This gives the meat a chance to reabsorb all the cooking juices.

For a Buffet

- Use height. A stack of old books (or a box or two) adds drama and elegance to your table.
- Place dishes at the beginning of the buffet and napkins and silverware at the end so guests are not juggling everything at once.
- Label your food so people know what they are eating.

Whole Roasted Filet with Blue Cheese Sauce

1 6 lb. filet roast, trimmed and tied

Kosher salt and fresh cracked pepper to taste

Season roast with salt and pepper 1 hour prior to cooking. Roast uncovered at 350º for 1 hour or until desired temperature is reached internally.

Medium-Rare 135º // Medium-Well 150º
Remember to let the meat rest 10-20 minutes before slicing.

Blue Cheese Sauce

1⁄2 cup sour cream

1⁄2 cup mayonnaise

1 cup crumbled blue cheese

Whisk together and serve cold.

When cooking a roast in the oven, check the internal temperature; the roast will continue to cook to about 5-10 more degrees after you take it out. The internal temperature will continue to rise while the meat is "resting."

FOR THE LOVE OF ITALY

The Italians are a pleasure to watch. You can get real entertainment hanging out a window and watching the action below. Hands and arms fly in every direction, kisses are given galore and voices are raised in a sing-song tone which makes you believe all is done with love and passion. They are handsome people, men debonair and aristocratic, and women, beautiful and sexy at any age, with an elegance that is born to them. They don't have to try; it is in their faces, eyes and gestures. I can't get enough. Italy is a way of life. We vacation there for a glimpse of all that is passion, hoping to take some home...memories, at least. It is a place to return to, a promise that all is well and that you can live with a zest for life, food and love.

TO DEGLAZE A PAN>> When browning meat in a sauté pan, little bits of seasoning will stick to the pan. This is where all the flavor is. Add any type of liquid (broth, wine, water) to gather all those browned and flavorful bits to make a tasty sauce for your meat.

Always use a dark speckled roasting pan. It promotes browning.

Three Bean Chili

- 5 lbs. ground beef
- 3 6-ounce cans tomato paste
- 3 6-ounce cans water
- 4 tablespoons Worcestershire sauce
- 1 1/2 cups diced onion
- 1 red pepper, seeded and diced
- 1 yellow pepper, seeded and diced
- 1 green pepper, seeded and diced
- 1 20-ounce can white beans, drained and rinsed
- 1 20-ounce can black beans, drained and rinsed
- 1 20-ounce can red beans, drained and rinsed
- 1 tablespoon hot sauce
- 4 cloves garlic, chopped
- 3 tablespoons chili powder
- 1-2 jalapeño peppers, diced (optional)
- Kosher salt and fresh cracked pepper to taste

Brown the ground beef and drain excess liquid. Mix with remaining ingredients and simmer 2-2 1/2 hours on top of the stove, or in a 350º oven, covered. Be sure to stir occasionally. Serve with chopped red onion, shredded cheese and corn bread.

Florentine Roast Chicken Rosemary

1 4-5 lb. roasting chicken
1 tablespoon dried rosemary
Kosher salt and fresh cracked pepper to taste
1⁄4 cup olive oil
1 tablespoon garlic (granulated)
6 whole cloves garlic
1 fresh sprig rosemary

Rinse chicken and pat dry. Rub with olive oil and season with salt, pepper, garlic and dried rosemary. Place whole garlic cloves and fresh rosemary in cavity of chicken. Roast uncovered at 350º for 1 to 1 1⁄4 hour or you can cheat and cook until the popper comes out! When the chicken is finished, add 8 ounces of water to drippings in roasting pan for a delicious au jus.

Granulated garlic, found in the spice section of your supermarket, has a sand-like texture and flavors meat wonderfully.

Chicken with Bourbon Dijon Sauce

2 lbs. boneless chicken breast
2 tablespoons butter
2 tablespoons olive oil
Kosher salt and fresh cracked pepper to taste

Cut chicken breast into scallops with sharp knife. Sauté lightly in butter and oil until lightly browned. Season with salt and pepper. Place sautéed chicken scallops in ovenproof pottery dish.

Make chicken scallops by slicing into the meat at an angle with a sharp knife. This should yield 2-3 scallops per breast.

Bourbon Sauce

1⁄2 cup Dijon mustard
1⁄2 cup brown sugar
1⁄2 cup bourbon
1 tablespoon Worcestershire sauce
Kosher salt and fresh cracked pepper to taste
1 10-ounce can cream of chicken soup

Combine ingredients in saucepan and simmer 10-15 minutes. Pour over sautéed chicken scallops and bake, covered, at 350º for 30-35 minutes.

When cooking, let your imagination run free. Be creative. Look at your food as an artist looks at her paints. Use bright colors and add pizazz to your plate!

Martini Chicken

2 lbs. boneless chicken breast
2 tablespoons butter
2 tablespoons olive oil
Kosher salt and fresh cracked pepper to taste

Cut chicken breast into scallops with sharp knife. Sauté lightly in butter and oil until lightly browned. Season with salt and pepper. Place sautéed chicken scallops in ovenproof pottery dish.

Martini Sauce

1/2 cup olive oil
3 shallots, chopped
3 cloves garlic, chopped
1/4 cup chopped pimento stuffed green olives
1/2 cup chicken broth
1/2 cup white vermouth
1 10-ounce can cream of chicken soup
1 tablespoon lemon juice
Kosher salt and fresh cracked pepper to taste

Sauté shallots, garlic and olives in hot oil until fragrant. Combine with remaining ingredients and cook until smooth. Pour over sautéed chicken scallops and bake covered at 350º for 30-35 minutes.

A shallot is small, like a head of garlic but with a brown, papery skin like an onion, yet is sweeter than either garlic or onion.

Chicken Piccatta

1 lb. boneless chicken breast
1 tablespoon butter
1 tablespoon olive oil
Kosher salt and fresh cracked pepper to taste

Cut chicken breast into scallops with a sharp knife. Sauté lightly in butter and oil until lightly browned. Season with salt and pepper. Place sautéed chicken scallops in ovenproof pottery dish.
USE SAME SAUTÉ PAN FOR SAUCE.

Piccatta Sauce

1 tablespoon olive oil
2 tablespoons butter
2 cloves garlic, chopped
1/2 cup white vermouth
1/4 cup lemon juice
1/2 cup chicken broth
1/4 cup capers
1/4 cup chopped Italian flat leaf parsley
Lemon slices for garnish

Sauté garlic in oil and butter until soft. Add remaining ingredients to deglaze the pan. Pour over sautéed chicken and bake covered at 350º for 30-35 minutes. Garnish with lemon slices.

A MUD BATH

Driving the highways that run through the Napa Valley in California is like eating antipasto, you try a little bit of this, a little bit of that. Hundreds of wineries are tucked into every corner, down an obscure gravel drive or up a sky tram to the top of a mountain. We had made frequent stops at these wineries, tasting the local varieties, so that by mid-afternoon we often forgot who and where we were.

Today is different. Today we have an agenda, and rolling, laying and squishing around in mud are on it. We follow more of the narrow, quiet roads just a few miles north to Calistoga and soon reach our destination, the original mud baths of northern California.

The scene that awaits us is quite different from what we had expected. The décor consists of cinder block walls and cold, concrete floors. There are no flowers or pictures on the walls; definitely not the typical "spa" comforts that we had anticipated.

Clint and I say our farewells for the next several hours as we head toward the separate men and women's quarters. I am escorted down a narrow hallway into a small changing room by a straight-faced, stone cold "drill sergeant" whom I aptly name Matilda. She hands me a towel the size of a postage stamp and instructs me to get undressed. I put my clothes in the locker. I am then led to a cavernous room with lots of running water, steam, mist and a faint smell of wet dirt. In the corner sit two gigantic tubs filled to the brim with what looks like wet mulch. Matilda tells me to get in. This maneuver is not going to be easy. The tubs are high on the platforms, steam sizzles from the surface. I am naked. The rim of these tubs is at least a foot wide. As I step into the tub, I think, "I paid for this?"

As I ease my way down to lie on the plank, Matilda is already covering me with mud. It is heavy and wet, hot and steamy, kind of smelly, but not repulsive. I lay back, my hands still clenching the sides of the tub, afraid I'll slip under.

Just as soon as I get my hands in the tub, covered in mud to my neck, my nose starts to itch. My eyes water, sweat runs down from my hairline.

"Twenty minutes," barks Matilda, as she places cucumber slices over my eyes and a cool washcloth over my head. I can do this.

Matilda periodically appears to check on my mud and me. Hot, steamy and heavy, yet my limbs feel weightless. I relax. She's back already? Matilda knows her job, the effect the mud has on people, and heaves me up and out with ease. Mud clings to my every pore and crack; how am I ever going to get all this off?

Able to cover only so much of myself with my little towel, I follow Matilda, past the other guests, to an open shower stall. She adjusts the water, hands me the nozzle and disappears.

I try to be graceful, bending and twisting so that the stream of water can loosen and flush the mud. I watch it slide down the drain and immediately feel 10 pounds lighter. I maneuver myself a little more; surely I must have all the mud off me.

Next I'm led to a whirlpool bath. The water is cool and fragrant, and the strategically placed jets help dislodge the last of the mud. Too soon again, I am helped out of the bath and handed warm towels. As a sauna door opens and the steam hisses, I realize I am not alone. Three naked women, pink and glistening, sit in silence and sweat. What could be next?

The masseuse leads me into a tiny room filled with candles, music and incense. She rubs me with fragrant oils and gives me a wonderful one-hour massage. She dims the lights, swaths me in warm towels and blankets, then leaves. I fall into oblivion.

My mud day is over. I meet Clint in the waiting room. He is pink, flushed and looking as refreshed as I feel. On weak knees, we leave feeling happy and relaxed.

Chicken with New Orleans Cream Sauce

1 lb. boneless chicken breast

1 tablespoon butter

1 tablespoon olive oil

Kosher salt and fresh cracked pepper to taste

Cut chicken breast into scallops with a sharp knife. Sauté lightly in butter and oil until lightly browned. Season with salt and pepper. Place sautéed chicken scallops in ovenproof pottery dish.

New Orleans Cream Sauce

4 tablespoons butter

1 tablespoon olive oil

2 shallots, chopped

6-8 garlic cloves, chopped

1⁄4 lb. smoked sausage, diced

1 teaspoon Worcestershire sauce

1 teaspoon hot sauce

1 tablespoon Creole seasoning

1 10-ounce can cream of chicken soup

1⁄2 cup heavy cream

Topping

1⁄2 cup grated Parmesan cheese

1⁄2 cup chopped scallion

Sauté shallots and garlic in butter and oil until fragrant. Add smoked sausage and brown for a few minutes then add remaining ingredients and cook until smooth. Pour over sautéed chicken scallops and top with Parmesan cheese and scallion. Bake covered at 350º for 20-25 minutes.

Chicken Italiano

4 lbs. assorted chicken pieces

1 cup flour

Kosher salt and fresh cracked pepper to taste

Vegetable oil for frying

Mix flour with salt and pepper. Dip chicken pieces in flour mix. Heat a sauté pan and then add the oil. Heat oil and fry chicken until crispy. (The chicken doesn't have to be completely cooked.) Remove and put chicken in ovenproof pottery. Top with sauce and bake covered at 350º for 35-40 minutes.

Sauce

1⁄4 cup olive oil

2 large onions, chopped

4 cloves garlic, chopped

2 red peppers, seeded and diced

2 green peppers, seeded and diced

Kosher salt and fresh cracked pepper to taste

2 cups marinara sauce

1⁄2 cup Marsala wine

Sauté onion, garlic and peppers in olive oil until fragrant. Season with salt and pepper. Add marinara sauce and Marsala. Cook uncovered 10-15 minutes.

Maple Glazed Roast Pork

4-5 lbs. boneless pork loin roast, tied

Rub pork with dry rub mixture and marinate up to 1 hour. Roast uncovered at 350º for 1 1⁄2 hours or until the internal temperature reads 150º. Cool and slice. Put roast back together. Just before serving pour glaze over roast and reheat in oven.

When ordering your pork roast, be sure to have the butcher tie the meat. Tying helps the roast cook evenly and not curl up when roasting.

Dry Rub

2 tablespoons dried rosemary

1 tablespoon granulated garlic

Kosher salt and fresh cracked pepper to taste

Combine ingredients in a bowl.

Glaze

1⁄2 cup olive oil

1 1⁄2 cups chopped onion

2 cups maple syrup

1⁄2 cup cider vinegar

3 tablespoons Dijon mustard

2 tablespoons dry mustard

Kosher salt and fresh cracked pepper

Mix ingredients in saucepan and bring to a boil. Reduce heat and simmer for 20 minutes to reduce liquid.

MY HOME—MY CASTLE

Sometimes I work so much that I really can't enjoy my home. I pass through without really noticing my surroundings. When I need to relax I go away for a few days, to another state, another country, another culture. But one August I was lucky enough to stop and enjoy my house, my garden, my plants and my pottery. Clint and I chose new colors for our walls—bold and beautiful. A new paint job freshens and enlightens the house. We poured over photos Clint took on our trips, selecting our favorites to frame and hang. We gardened, pulled weeds, harvested tomatoes, watered the flowers and fed the birds. We sat on the porch at sunset with a glass of wine as we listened to the locusts and waved to our neighbors.

I love my house. I'm surrounded by photos and moments of my life. I feel comfortable and serene here. It is a home where family gathers and friends visit. Food is always shared along with laughter and tears. Make your house a home, a gathering place for laughter and love. It will be both a fortress and a soft place in your life.

Ham and Cabbage

6 slices bacon, cut up

2 tablespoons butter

2 tablespoons olive oil

2 cloves garlic, chopped

1 1⁄2 cups chopped onion

2 tablespoons brown sugar

1⁄4 cup cider vinegar

1 tablespoon Dijon mustard

1 teaspoon celery seed

1 cup chicken broth

Kosher salt and fresh cracked pepper to taste

2 heads cabbage, washed and cut up

2 ham butts, cut into cubes

In large ovenproof pot, cook bacon and drain off half of drippings. Add butter and oil. Sauté garlic and onion until golden. Add remaining ingredients and mix well. Cover and roast at 350º for 2-2 1⁄2 hours.

SOARING

The glider office was in a trailer on the edge of a huge field. We entered the trailer and met the owner, president and pilot of the plane parked in the distance. We chose our flight options and completed some forms. The very first question on one form asked for height and weight. Weight? From my point of view, this question is worse than asking someone's age. Even though I knew it was important to answer this question truthfully, years of lying about my weight took over. Clint and I each miraculously lost 10 pounds. With our lies documented on paper, we were about to get the thrill of a lifetime.

Up close, the plane looked less sturdy than it had from afar. It was light green, the color of those old wooden stalls that sold ice cream on the beach. Extra long wings extended from the cockpit. There were two seats directly behind one another, a small dashboard with controls in front. I felt a familiar flutter in my stomach, the one that often happens when I'm waiting to enter a wild amusement ride. The cockpit looked too small for three adults. The pilot took the front seat. Clint and I wedged our way into the back seat. Then I understood why they wanted our weight. Suitably squashed, I noticed that our plane was attached by a rope to another larger plane in front of us.

The larger plane took off first and since we were tied together, we weren't far behind. Off we went toward the mountains. The plane in front of us, the one towing us, the one with the engine, suddenly dropped its line, literally, and we were on our own, gliding in the air currents. It was both exhilarating and frightening, especially when the pilot turned completely around from the controls to inform us we were soaring at 1,000 feet in the air.

Although my fists were clenched and my heart fluttering, I could truly appreciate the magnificent sights. Below us were the vineyards of Napa Valley, each winery distinct in its layout. The houses and farms looked tiny from our vantage point. In the distance we could see hot air balloons floating through the brilliant blue sky. We were soaring like birds across invisible sheets of air; we glided more than we flew. I was finally able to relax and enjoy the spectacular view.

I realized that the little lies about our weight must have been expected and that we were, thankfully, not in any danger. And then I thought about the landing. I remembered seeing only one small wheel as landing gear. I became nervous. No need to worry. The pilot had done this many times before. Smooth landing to a fabulous ride.

Voodoo Pork

2 packages pork tenderloins

Pork tenderloins usually come two to a package, each tenderloin weighing about one pound. With this recipe, you should have four pieces. Remove meat from packaging. Rinse tenderloins and pat dry. Season with salt and pepper. Roast uncovered at 350º for 20 minutes on a baking pan sprayed with cooking spray. Cool and slice. Just before serving, top with sauce and bake covered for 15-20 minutes or until hot.

Voodoo Sauce

1/2 cup ketchup

1/2 cup cider vinegar

1/2 cup apple juice

1 cup hot pepper jelly

1 teaspoon honey

1 teaspoon garlic powder

Kosher salt and fresh cracked pepper to taste

Simmer all ingredients in saucepan 15-20 minutes or until flavors blend. Pour over cooked tenderloins.

Salt or dry rub your meat 1 hour before you roast it for a delicious flavor.

Roast Pork Italian Style "Porchette"

Porchette is traditionally a whole roasted pig studded with garlic cloves and sprinkled lavishly with rosemary. This is a pared down "at home" version, still tantalizingly delicious.

4-5 lb. pork loin roast, tied

2 tablespoons dried rosemary

1 tablespoon granulated garlic

Kosher salt and fresh cracked pepper to taste

1 teaspoon cayenne pepper

2 tablespoons chopped Italian flat leaf parsley

6-8 whole cloves of garlic

3-4 tablespoons olive oil

1-1 1/2 cups water or white wine (to be added during cooking)

With a paring knife make small pockets in the meat and insert whole garlic cloves. Rub pork with olive oil. Mix rosemary, granulated garlic, salt, pepper, cayenne and parsley. Rub herb mixture on both sides of roast. Roast uncovered at 350º for 1 1/2 hours or until internal temperature reads 150º. Add water or wine half way through cooking time to make a wonderful au jus.

Add water or wine to the bottom of your roasting pan when the roast starts to brown. Waiting this 30 or 40 minutes into the roasting time helps make a flavorful au jus.

Honey Creole Pork Tenderloins

2 packages pork tenderloins (4 pieces)

2 tablespoons Creole seasoning

Kosher salt and fresh cracked pepper to taste

Rinse tenderloins and pat dry. Season with salt, pepper and seasoning. Roast uncovered at 350º for 20 minutes. Cool and slice.

Sauce

1 cup Dijon mustard

2 tablespoons Creole seasoning

1/2 cup honey

1/2 cup brown sugar

1/2 cup cider vinegar

Kosher salt and fresh cracked pepper to taste

Combine all ingredients in saucepan and simmer 15-20 minutes until blended. Pour over cooked pork tenderloins. Reheat covered at 350º for 15-20 minutes or until hot.

When serving a roast for a party, I like to cook it first, let it cool and then slice it. I put the sliced roast back together and then reheat it with a sauce. The meat is easier to serve to a crowd if it is already sliced.

South Carolina Barbecue

I love going to NASCAR races in the south. There are barbeque places on every corner. Family owned, each holds their recipes in high esteem. It's all very delicious and finger-licking good!

2 1/2 - 3 1/2 lbs. pork shoulder

Dry Rub

1 teaspoon salt

1 teaspoon pepper

1 teaspoon chili powder

1 teaspoon granulated garlic

Combine all ingredients. Rub onto the pork shoulder 1 hour prior to cooking.

Sauce

1/4 cup Worcestershire sauce

1/4 cup red wine vinegar

Dash hot pepper sauce

4 cups ketchup

1/4 cup brown sugar

1 teaspoon paprika

1 tablespoon Dijon mustard

Kosher salt and fresh cracked pepper to taste

1 cup root beer soda

Combine all ingredients in a saucepan and simmer for 10-15 minutes. Pour sauce over pork shoulder. Roast covered at 350º for 2-2 1/2 hours. Cool and shred meat.

Southwestern Pork Tenderloin with Fabulous Barbecue Sauce

This is a great barbeque sauce for chicken and ribs, too!

2 packages pork tenderloins (4 pieces)

Rinse tenderloins and pat dry.

Dry Rub

1 teaspoon chili powder

1 teaspoon salt

1 teaspoon pepper

1 teaspoon garlic powder

Combine ingredients and rub on pork tenderloins 1 hour prior to cooking. Roast uncovered at 350º for 20 minutes. Cool and slice.

Barbeque Sauce

1 cup ketchup

Dash hot sauce

1 tablespoon Worcestershire sauce

1 teaspoon celery seeds

1⁄2 cup water

Kosher salt and fresh cracked pepper to taste

1 tablespoon brown sugar

Combine ingredients in saucepan and simmer for 15-20 minutes. Pour over cooked pork tenderloins. Reheat covered at 350º for 15-20 minutes or until hot.

Sugar Glazed Baked Ham with Peach Chutney

Have your butcher slice the ham for buffet and tie it back together. Most markets will do this for free. It makes for easy entertaining!

1 whole boneless ham

Glaze

4 tablespoons brown sugar

1 8-ounce jar chutney

1 8-ounce jar peach preserves

1 tablespoon Dijon mustard

Combine all ingredients to make a paste. Pour over tied ham and bake uncovered at 350º for 1 hour or until warmed. Serve with peachy Dijon mustard.

Peachy Dijon Mustard

1 cup Dijon mustard

2-3 tablespoons peach preserves

Combine and serve on side with ham and miniature rolls for sandwiches.

Me First!

It's important to take care of yourself. We put everyone first saving little time for ourselves in a busy day. If you are tired, stressed and always the last in your household to get any time and attention, it's easy to become resentful and angry. When my life gets crazy, I always remember that when you are sitting on an airplane waiting for take off, a flight attendant demonstrates the use of emergency exits and oxygen masks and explains, "If you are traveling with someone who needs assistance, put your oxygen mask on first and then tend to them." Use that information in your daily life. Take care of yourself and then you are better equipped to take care of others!

We live in a busy and stressful world, accomplishing task after task without stopping to smell the roses. Make a special effort to spend some time with your family and friends. It's what life is all about!

Call on God but row away from the rocks. — Indian Proverb

Growing up Italian, plastic was everywhere—on the lamp shade, sofa and even the pathway from the front door! They were saving it—for what I don't know. Everyday is a special occasion.

PASTA

Keep it Clean

- To remove a stain from a glass or bottle, fill with water and drop in two denture cleaning tablets.
- To clean tarnished gold or silver, rub with a paste of water and baking soda.

***PASTA SECRET* >>** *If you add 2-3 tablespoons water from boiling pasta to your sauces, they will become silkier and smoother.*

Pasta with Shrimp, Aglio & Olio
(Pasta with Shrimp, Garlic and Oil)

2 lbs. frozen cooked and cleaned shrimp, defrosted and drained well

3/4 cup olive oil

3-4 cloves garlic, minced

1 teaspoon hot pepper flakes

1 tablespoon chopped Italian flat leaf parsley

Kosher salt and fresh cracked pepper to taste

1/2 cup grated Parmesan cheese

1 lb. pasta, cooked and drained (reserve 1/2 cup pasta water)

Sauté garlic, parsley and red pepper flakes in hot oil. Toss with shrimp and add pasta water. Season with salt and pepper. Toss with pasta and cheese.

If your family is like mine, they love to pick out the shrimp and then all you have left is the pasta! If it's like this in your home, just double the amount of shrimp in the recipe. I always use large shrimp (26/30 count) which means there are 26 to 30 shrimp to a pound.

Tortellini with Ham and Peas in a Creamy Parmesan Sauce

1 lb. tri-colored tortellini, cooked and drained (reserve 2-3 tablespoons pasta water for sauce)

3 tablespoons butter

2 tablespoons olive oil

1 red pepper, seeded and chopped

1 large onion, chopped (1 1/2 cups)

1 cup chopped ham

2 cups frozen peas, defrosted

1 cup heavy cream

1/2 cup chicken broth

1/2 cup grated Parmesan cheese

Kosher salt and fresh cracked pepper to taste

Sauté pepper and onion in butter and oil until soft, about 10 minutes. Add ham and peas and cook until golden, about 10 minutes more. Add remaining ingredients and season with salt and pepper. Toss pasta with this mixture and sprinkle with grated Parmesan cheese.

I sometimes use tavern-style ham, available at your local deli, for recipes that include cooked ham.

Spicy Marinara with Chunky Zucchini

3 tablespoons olive oil
2 tablespoons butter
1 1/2 cups chopped onion
1 yellow squash, chopped (about 1 cup)
1 zucchini, chopped (about 1 cup)
1 red pepper, seeded and chopped
2-3 cloves garlic, chopped
1 Italian hot pepper, chopped
2 tablespoons chopped fresh basil
Kosher salt and cracked pepper to taste
1 teaspoon red pepper flakes
2 cups marinara sauce
1 lb. pasta, cooked and drained (reserve 2-3 tablespoons pasta water)
1/2 cup grated Parmesan cheese

Sauté all vegetables in butter and oil for 10 minutes, stirring occasionally. Season with salt, pepper, hot pepper flakes and basil. Add marinara and pasta water and cook 5-10 additional minutes. Toss with cooked pasta and top with 1/2 cup grated Parmesan cheese.

I like to use a combination of butter and olive oil in my cooking. Olive oil is good for you and butter tastes great! A wonderful combination.

THE GARLIC QUEEN

Walking along the streets of Amsterdam is like taking in a show. Stylishly dressed people walk briskly or stroll hand in hand. Bicycles come at you from all directions, bells chiming as they pass. Tulips and daffodils are on every corner, window box and step. The boat traffic in the canal is brisk, the bridges lit by twinkling lights. It is a surreal and exciting city.

As we wander, casually looking for a place to have dinner, we find ourselves on a little back street right behind the bloemenmarkt (a market where spring flowers and every variety of tulip are displayed in a riot of color). We are on a tiny street that has restaurants one after another, a culinary delight. We want something different, something exciting, adventurous, some place stimulating to eat. "The Garlic Queen" is just ahead.

We are greeted at the door by a man dressed in a royal blue jacket that resembles a costume from elegant days of kings and queens. The dining room is awash in jewel colors of royal blue, deep red, luscious green. Candles and candelabras are everywhere. The centerpieces for the tables are crowns, their jewels twinkling in the lights of flickering candles. The place is packed. We are seated at a window table; perfect for watching the wonders of Amsterdam pass by in the street.

First course is the whole baked head of garlic, swimming in a delicious seasoned olive oil accompanied by crisp warm bread for dunking. The garlic soup, creamy and delicious is followed by prawns sautéed with garlic and herbs, then beef stew with what must be 60 cloves of garlic, more bread, wonderful garlic mashed potatoes, green beans drizzled with carmelized garlic, salad with deep fried garlic chips crowning crisp greens.

We can't decide on dessert so we order one of each special: an out-of-this-world creamy vanilla ice cream made with cardamom and exotic spices and a rich gooey, caramel tart. We have our coffee and loosen our pants, but the meal's not over yet. Our waiter comes bearing two tiny dishes, each containing a piece of chocolate candy filled with a sweet, creamy garlic center. Heaven. This was an adventure I'll never forget.

Pasta with Shrimp and Spinach in a Creamy Garlic Sauce

1 lb. pasta, cooked and drained (reserve 2-3 tablespoons of pasta water)

2 lbs. frozen cooked and cleaned shrimp, defrosted and drained well

6 tablespoons butter

1 tablespoon chopped garlic

3 cups baby spinach leaves

1 cup heavy cream

1⁄2 cup chicken broth

1⁄2 cup grated Parmesan cheese

Kosher salt and fresh cracked pepper to taste

Sauté garlic in butter. Add cream, chicken broth and pasta water. Season with salt and pepper. Simmer for 10 minutes. Add shrimp and toss sauce with pasta and baby spinach. (The spinach will wilt from the heat of the pasta and sauce.) Top with Parmesan cheese.

Penne with Asparagus in Blush Sauce

1 lb. penne pasta, cooked and drained (reserve 2-3 tablespoons pasta water)

1 lb. asparagus, cut on an angle

2 cups marinara sauce

1⁄3 cup heavy cream

1⁄3 cup chicken broth

1⁄4 cup grated Parmesan cheese

Kosher salt and fresh cracked pepper to taste

During the last 5 minutes of boiling, add the asparagus to the pasta water to cook. Drain and then toss with remaining ingredients. Season with salt and pepper.

PASTA SECRET >> *When cooking pasta I bring cold water to a boil, throw in pasta and stir immediately until pasta begins to float around in the water, about 3-4 minutes. When pasta is finished you can check doneness by tasting a piece or as the old Italian saying goes, 'throw it against the wall and if it sticks you know it's done!' Pasta often sticks together as soon as you drain it because starch is released during cooking. After draining, do not rinse—this will allow the sauce or dressing to stick to the pasta nicely. Toss pasta with a small amount of olive oil and salt. If the pasta is for a salad stir occasionally until cool. Then add remaining ingredients. If it will be served hot, immediately toss with sauce and serve.*

Pasta Amatriciana

This is one of Clint's favorite dishes!

3 tablespoons butter

3 tablespoons olive oil

1 1⁄2 cups chopped onion

3 cloves garlic, minced

1 teaspoon red pepper flakes

1⁄2 lb. proscuitto, chopped

Kosher salt and fresh cracked pepper to taste

2 cups marinara sauce

1⁄2 cup grated Parmesan cheese

1 lb. pasta cooked and drained (reserve 2-3 tablespoons pasta water)

Sauté onion, garlic and red pepper flakes in butter and oil until golden, 5-10 minutes. Add chopped proscuitto and cook until browned, 10 minutes more. Add reserved pasta water and simmer. Top cooked pasta and sprinkle with cheese.

Proscuitto is a cured Italian ham. It is sliced very, very thin—you can almost see through it. The domestic has less fat than the imported. In the U.S. we are always trying to stay away from fat, but the Italians know that fat equals flavor.

Pasta with Broccoli and Golden Garlic

- 1 lb. pasta, cooked and drained (reserve 2-3 tablespoons pasta water)
- 2 heads broccoli, cut up
- 3⁄4 cup olive oil
- 3 tablespoons butter, melted
- 10 gloves garlic, whole
- 1⁄2 cup chicken broth
- 1⁄2 cup grated Parmesan cheese
- Kosher salt and fresh cracked pepper to taste

Cook broccoli in boiling water until bright green and tender. Drain. Sauté garlic cloves in butter and oil until golden, about 15 minutes. Add broccoli, chicken broth and pasta water and toss with pasta. Season with salt and pepper and top with Parmesan cheese.

Marinara Sauce

I use this sauce as a base for all my pasta sauces, as well as soups and stews. It's easy, wonderful and delicious!

- 1⁄2 cup olive oil
- 2-3 tablespoons butter
- 1 large onion, chopped fine (1 1⁄2 cups)
- 4 cloves garlic, chopped
- 4-6 tablespoons shredded fresh basil
- 2-3 tablespoons chopped Italian flat leaf parsley
- Kosher salt and fresh cracked pepper to taste
- 1 teaspoon sugar
- 2 29-ounce cans chef cut tomatoes or plum tomatoes chopped up with liquid
- 1-2 tablespoons tomato paste

Sauté onion and garlic in oil and butter until golden over medium heat for 10-15 minutes. Add basil, parsley, salt, pepper and sugar. Cook 5-10 minutes. Add canned tomatoes and tomato paste. Bring to a simmer and cook at least 30-40 minutes over low heat.

MY MOTHER'S HANDS

I have a tendency to freeze myself at a certain age and only when someone (usually my sister) not so gently reminds me of how old I am, do I realize, wow, middle age is setting in. Now, don't get me wrong. I'll be the first and loudest to say that I love my life.

It's better as you get older. It's easier somehow. Certain things start to happen—like when you're talking to your kids and your mother's words come out of your mouth. Oh, no! I thought I'd never say that. But there it is, and you know, it sounds pretty good.

I recently spent a day cooking with my mom. We hadn't been in the kitchen together for a long time. I remember about when, as a child, I had watched her make homemade pasta. She would turn a mountain of flour and a few eggs into silky strands of pasta that were left to dry on the kitchen table while we went to church. She rolled the dough so fast making gnocchi that I wanted to record it all on a slow motion camera so I could see just exactly how she did it. Flour was spread on the table and little bundles of pasta were neat in a row.

That day, as my mom and I were cooking together, rolling out dough, hands covered with flour, I looked down at my hands. There I saw my mother's hands, which looked pretty good to me!

PASTA SECRET >> *When making pasta dishes ahead of time, reheat using a little chicken broth if pasta mixture gets too thick.*

Penne with Ricotta Sauce

1 lb. penne pasta, cooked and drained (reserve 2-3 tablespoons pasta water)

1⁄4 cup olive oil

1 1⁄2 cups whole milk ricotta cheese

1 1⁄2 cups light cream

1 cup marinara sauce

1⁄2 cup grated Parmesan cheese

Kosher salt and fresh cracked pepper to taste

As soon as pasta is cooked, drain it but keep 2-3 tablespoons pasta water aside. Toss the pasta with the olive oil and season with salt and pepper. While pasta is still hot, gently fold in ricotta cheese, pasta water and cream. It should incorporate easily if pasta is hot. Add marinara sauce and top with Parmesan cheese.

You can find fresh ricotta cheese at a pasta shop or cheese store. It is incredibly delicious!

Pasta Piselli (Pasta and Peas)

Ditalini pasta or tubetti pasta work well with this dish!

3-4 tablespoons olive oil

3 tablespoons butter

4 cloves garlic, chopped

1 1⁄2 cups chopped onion

2 cups frozen peas, defrosted

2 cups marinara sauce

1⁄4 cup chicken broth

1⁄2 cup grated Parmesan cheese

1 lb. pasta, cooked and drained (reserve 2-3 tablespoons pasta water)

Kosher salt and fresh cracked pepper to taste

Sauté garlic and onion in oil and butter until golden, 5-10 minutes. Add peas along with marinara, pasta water and broth. Season with salt and pepper. Toss with pasta and top with Parmesan cheese.

PASTA SECRET >> *It's important to marry your pasta with your sauce. For example, don't use a thin pasta like capellini with a heavy sauce made with ricotta. It overwhelms the pasta. Heavy sauces go with a larger or thicker strand of pasta and light sauces with a small or thin pasta. A match made in pasta heaven!*

Pasta with Vodka Sauce

5 tablespoons butter, melted

1 teaspoon hot pepper flakes

2⁄3 cup vodka

2 cups marinara sauce

1⁄2 cup heavy cream

Kosher salt and fresh cracked pepper to taste

1 lb. pasta, cooked and drained (reserve 2-3 tablespoons pasta water)

1⁄2 cup grated Parmesan cheese

Melt butter. Add hot pepper flakes and vodka. (Be sure to turn the heat low when adding vodka, the alcohol is highly flammable.) Cook a few minutes and then add marinara sauce, pasta water and cream. Season with salt and pepper. Toss with pasta and cheese.

When using a liquor or wine in cooking, remember to use the best. What you put into your cooking is what you get out of it. We are worth it! Good rule: If you don't like to drink it—don't cook with it!

GROWING UP ITALIAN

I grew up in an Italian neighborhood, a miniature Italian village in West Philadelphia. All sights, sounds, foods, music, thoughts and ideas were Italian. The grade school that I attended for eight years required that at least one parent be of Italian decent. Most children spoke the language. Traditions were steeped in history. Food played a major role. Little corner stores carried all of the makings of a festive Italian dinner—proscuitto, salami, sharp cheeses, olives, broccoli rabe, chicory, savory cabbage, fresh figs, homemade ricotta and grated Parmesan cheese. The butchers had saw dust on the floor and penned lambs outside during the Easter holidays. The chicken man had rows of cages with every possible kind of live fowl.

I accompanied my mother on many shopping excursions. I was there as she bargained with the purveyors, trying for the best possible selections at the best price. I sat in the kitchen on Saturday mornings as my mom, like countless other Italian mothers, made her gravy in preparation for Sunday dinner, to be served right after Mass. The wonderful aromas would simmer through the house. Mom would fry her meatballs and we would eat them right out of the frying pan, hot and tasty. Bracciole, a piece of pork and sometimes chicken, would accompany the meatballs floating in gravy. Sunday dinner couldn't come fast enough.

Early on Sunday morning, my mother would make the "homemades." This was pasta from scratch, the dough mixed early in the morning, resting in a dusting of flour on a wooden board and covered with a dish towel. Pasta machine ready, attached to the kitchen table, we children would help her roll out the dough. Ribbons of golden pasta whirled out of that machine again and again, until it was paper thin and ready to be cut into macaroni. We didn't call it pasta back then.

The strands of pasta lay drying on the kitchen table while we went to Mass. Saint Donato's was right up the street. Upstairs in the big church Mass was in English, but downstairs in the chapel, Italian flowed like music to my ears. Everyone congregated outside to talk and then we were off to the local bakery for our Sunday pastry. A long line snaked out of the bakery door. We anticipated our selections of creamy cannoli, soft and soggy drenched Babba Rhum, and flaky, crisp sfogliatelle, filled with ricotta. The boxes of sweets were tied with string. Our mouths watered all the way home; the Sunday feast was only a few hours away.

This is the way we ate every Sunday—a tradition. We ate as a family in the dining room reserved for Sundays and holidays, and we ate very well indeed. I cherish my Italian upbringing. It has filled me with many memories, and made family and food an important part of my life.

Bay Leaves

The warming aroma of bay leaves is particularly appealing. The first Christians simmered bay leaves in their homes for a spicy and festive Christmas. In Morocco, bay leaves are used to line the cooking vessel in which the tiny pasta couscous is steamed. You can reduce salt in your recipes and substitute one bay leaf for each teaspoon of salt when cooking grains, rice and beans.

Make an herb vinegar with bay leaf, dried sage and red wine vinegar or tuck bay leaves into your centerpiece for a wonderful seasonal aroma.

Pasta with Crabmeat

This is a fast and delicious meal!

1 lb. jumbo lump crabmeat
2 tablespoons butter, melted
2 tablespoons olive oil
3 cloves garlic, chopped
1 teaspoon Old Bay seasoning
1 teaspoon hot sauce
1 teaspoon red pepper flakes
1⁄2 cup chicken broth
2 cups marinara sauce
1 lb. pasta, cooked and drained (reserve 2-3 tablespoons pasta water)
1⁄2 cup grated Parmesan cheese

Sauté garlic in butter and oil with Old Bay seasoning, hot sauce and pepper flakes. Add crabmeat, chicken broth and pasta water. Cook 5 minutes and then add marinara. Cook until blended, about 10 minutes, and toss with pasta and cheese.

Many Italians don't like to use grated cheese on pasta made with any kind of seafood. But I say do what you want. I love cheese so I always add it! And drink red wine with your seafood if you want.

Pasta Bologenese

A meal unto itself, this dish is rich and satisfying. You need only add a salad, Italian bread and wine for a fabulous feast.

1⁄2 cup olive oil
2 tablespoons butter, melted
2 lbs. ground mix (beef, pork and veal)
1 large onion, chopped (1 1/2 cups)
2-3 cloves garlic, chopped
Kosher salt and fresh cracked pepper to taste
1 bay leaf
1⁄2 cup chopped Italian flat leaf parsley
1⁄2 cup chicken broth
2 cups marinara sauce
1 lb. pasta, cooked and drained (reserve 2-3 tablespoons pasta water)
1⁄2 cup grated Parmesan cheese

Sauté onion and garlic in butter and oil 5-10 minutes. Add ground mix and stir until meat is browned and crumbly. Season with salt and pepper. Add chicken broth, pasta water, marinara sauce and bay leaf. Simmer 20-25 minutes. Remove bay leaf. Add parsley and toss with pasta. Top with Parmesan cheese.

Bay leaves add a wonderful flavor to your cooking, but be sure to remove them when you are serving your food. They are not pleasant to chew!

Instead of using dry boxed pasta, find a pasta store and purchase fresh pasta for your next meal. You will marvel at the difference it makes—silky and smooth. Homemade pasta is light as a feather and so delicious. And it cooks in less time, too!

Lobster Ravioli with Creamy Crab Sauce

1 lb. lobster ravioli, cooked and drained (reserve 2-3 tablespoons pasta water and toss ravioli with 1-2 tablespoons olive oil or butter to prevent them from sticking)

2 tablespoons butter, melted

2 tablespoons olive oil

2 cloves garlic, minced

1 shallot, chopped

1⁄4 cup chopped Italian flat leaf parsley

1 lb. jumbo lump crabmeat

Kosher salt and fresh ground pepper to taste

1 1⁄2 cups heavy cream

1⁄2 cup grated Parmesan cheese

Sauté garlic and shallot in butter and oil until soft. Add parsley and crabmeat. Season with salt and pepper. Cook 5-10 minutes. Add pasta water and heavy cream. Cook until warmed through, then pour over cooked ravioli. Top with Parmesan cheese.

You can find lobster ravioli at your local Italian market or pasta shop.

Gnocchi Verde

I love these light little gnocchi. I can eat them all day long!

2 10-ounce boxes frozen chopped spinach; defrost, drain and squeeze dry

1 cup whole milk ricotta cheese

2 eggs

2⁄3 cup grated Parmesan cheese

Kosher salt and fresh cracked pepper to taste

Pinch nutmeg

1 cup flour (more if necessary)

4 tablespoons butter, melted

1⁄2 cup grated Parmesan cheese

It is very important that the spinach be squeezed dry. Add to ricotta cheese, then add eggs, Parmesan, salt, pepper and nutmeg. Gradually add flour. Mixture should be sticky. Mix very well and refrigerate 20 minutes.

Roll into walnut size balls. Drop into boiling water. When they float to the top, remove with a slotted spoon to a pretty pottery baking dish. Drizzle with melted butter and cheese. Bake at 350º for 15-20 minutes.

When cooking (not baking) you can always substitute brown sugar or honey for regular sugar in a recipe. It gives food a wonderful flavor.

WALKING

- *Recharges and invigorates your body with extra intake of oxygen.*
- *Helps release muscle tension and facilitates blood circulation.*
- *Picking up the pace helps you feel more energetic and speeds up your thinking process and problem solving.*
- *Releases blocked energy, negative feelings and thoughts.*

Ask for divine intervention in the midst of a problem or upsetting situation.

Whether I am setting a table for 100 or just eating breakfast all by myself, I take the time to set the table using my favorite dishes and silverware and light a candle. These little touches make the difference. Treat yourself good. Never eat standing up and don't eat out of plastic containers. Give yourself the love and courtesy you give to all your family and guests. Don't wait for someone to buy you flowers—buy them for yourself. Do it for you! Eat off the GOOD china; everyday. Life is too short not to.

Smile

Laughter is the best medicine. Along with confidence, love, health and of course, long legs, I always wish for a sense of humor. I think laughter gets us through life and difficult situations better that anything else. If you can laugh and smile everyday all things seem possible. Try it, smile at people, at yourself and take life on the light side. It's so much easier!

SEAFOOD

CLEAR IT OUT

Leading a cluttered life is restricting. If you can't fit another thing into your closet or drawer, how can you go get some new stuff? When your life is so busy that you have absolutely no time for anything new, your life is in a rut.

This year I decided to make room in my drawers, closets, corners and calendar. I needed space. Everything was just too crowded. I lived and worked in an over-booked world. So I set a goal, putting aside time every day to go through a different space in my life to de-clutter, clear out and open things up. Then I felt I could breathe again.

It started small, in little spaces that were overtaking a room; old magazines, my t-shirt collection, my junk jewelry box. Then I went onto my closets and shoes. This was the hard part. Although my favorite shoes were probably only worn once or twice for really short periods (they killed my feet) I was in love with them. I made some concessions, giving away beige pumps but keeping my plum boots. Suddenly I feel lighter, better, more creative and not so crowded. More new things are coming my way and I feel the room to move around.

Take a look around you. It doesn't take long to simplify your life, and the rewards are lasting and relieving. Give some stuff away; make room for the new you.

"Martini" Salmon

1 side of salmon—skin removed
(approx. 3-3 1/2 lbs.)
2 tablespoons butter, melted
2 tablespoons olive oil
1 small red onion (about 1/2 cup), chopped
3-4 cloves garlic, chopped
1/2 cup chopped pimento stuffed green olives
2 tablespoons chopped Italian flat leaf parsley
3 tablespoons gin
1 teaspoon white vermouth
1/2 cup heavy cream
Kosher salt and fresh cracked pepper to taste

Sauté onion, garlic, olives and parsley in butter and oil until fragrant. Season with salt and pepper. Add gin and vermouth. Cook for an additional 5-10 minutes. Add cream. Turn off heat. Place salmon in an ovenproof pottery dish. Pour mixture evenly over salmon. Roast uncovered in a 350º oven for 20-25 minutes. Serve hot.

For a delicious and different flavor, substitute light or dark vermouth, Marsala, or Madeira in a recipe that calls for white wine.

Mussels with Sambuca and Cream

2 lbs. mussels, scrubbed and cleaned
2 tablespoons olive oil
2 cloves garlic, minced
4 tablespoons sambuca liqueur
1/4 cup heavy cream
1/2 cup chopped scallion
1/4 cup chopped Italian flat leaf parsley
Kosher salt and fresh cracked pepper to taste

In large sauté pan, heat garlic and oil. Add mussels. Cover and shake pan frequently until mussels open. Add sambuca, cream, scallion and parsley. Season with salt and pepper. Serve with plenty of bread or a spoon to mop up all the juices.

To clean mussels and clams, add 1-2 tablespoons of flour or cornmeal and cover with cold water. Rinse well, 2-3 times.

Roasted Salmon with Wasabi Pea Crust

1 side of salmon—skin removed (approx. 3-3 1/2 lbs.)
3-4 tablespoons butter, melted
1 tablespoon wasabi powder
1 cup crushed wasabi peas

Mix melted butter and wasabi powder together and brush onto the salmon. Crush wasabi peas in a food processor. Spread on top of salmon. Roast salmon uncovered at 350º for 25-30 minutes. Garnish with 1/4 cup chopped scallions.

Wasabi Sauce

1/2 cup sour cream
1/2 cup mayonnaise
2 tablespoons wasabi powder
2 tablespoons water
Kosher salt and fresh cracked pepper to taste

Mix sour cream and mayonnaise until blended. Mix wasabi powder and water to make a paste. Blend wasabi paste with sour cream and mayonnaise. Season with salt and pepper. Serve on side of roasted salmon.

When using butter to cook, always melt the butter first before adding other ingredients. The food will cook faster and more evenly.

Always use fresh garlic. Chop peeled garlic in a food processor covered with some extra virgin olive oil and kosher salt. It should last up to two weeks in the refrigerator. You can find peeled garlic cloves in most supermarket produce sections.

Pacific Rim Baked Fish

1 lb. white fish filet such as flounder or tilapia
1 tablespoon olive oil
1 tablespoon butter, melted
1 teaspoon minced ginger
2 cloves garlic, minced
1/4 cup soy sauce or teriyaki sauce
2 tablespoons lime juice
1 tablespoon brown sugar
1/4 cup chopped scallions
Kosher salt and fresh cracked pepper to taste

Briefly sauté ginger and garlic in butter and oil until fragrant, 5-10 minutes. Add remaining ingredients and pour over fish filet. Bake uncovered at 350º for 20 minutes. Garnish with fresh chopped scallion.

Buy only as much ginger as you need and break off what you want to use. Store remaining ginger in a jar of white wine in the refrigerator. To use, peel ginger with a small knife or ginger peeler, then chop in a food processor. Ginger should not be chopped until ready to use.

Ginger Chili Shrimp

This can be served as an appetizer or over rice for an entrée.

2 lbs. cooked and cleaned shrimp
1/2 cup olive oil
1 tablespoon hot sauce
2 tablespoons chopped ginger
3 cloves garlic, minced
1 tablespoon sesame oil
2 tablespoons soy sauce
1 teaspoon seafood seasoning
1/2 cup chopped scallions
Kosher salt and fresh cracked pepper to taste

Combine all ingredients, except shrimp, and sauté over a low flame until fragrant. Add shrimp, tossing well. Top with scallions.

FRIDAY FOODS

Italian meals and traditions are governed strongly by religion and economies. We were not allowed to eat meat on Fridays. This was a Catholic rule. More than one generation typically lived in a household. We lived with our parents and grandparents. Assisted living was not an option. The women would prepare the meal, serve it and then clean up while the men sat on the porch to relax.

Fridays had a special significance. Whether it was because the women wanted some time off from the drudgery in the kitchen, or the church forbade meat, Friday's meal was less formal and more fun.

Sometimes we had pizza. A bakery run out of the basement of a home had a reputation for wonderful thick crust tomato pie, basically pizza dough with gravy on top. We sprinkled on Parmesan cheese and red pepper flakes or spicy fried hots (long Italian peppers fried in oil and garlic until crisp and slightly burned). The alternative, white pie, was delicious in its simplicity of pizza dough rubbed with olive oil, garlic, salt and pepper. These square pizzas were wrapped in brown paper and brought home hot. They didn't sit around long before being devoured.

Another Friday dinner was frittata, a big fluffy omelet made with at least two dozen eggs beaten with a little water. My favorite was cooked with crisp, golden squares of potato fried in oil, then salted and added to the omelet. Other options were asparagus, peppers, even sliced tomatoes. With a fresh salad of chicory, arugula or other wild greens dressed in only vinegar and oil and, of course, a wedge of sharp provolone cheese, it was a simple but elegant feast.

My mother was a magician in the kitchen. It was hard not to pay attention to the aromas and flavors that she presented to us. Polenta, now considered by many a gourmet food, was a poor man's dish that was my all time favorite. Finely ground corn meal cooked long and slow until rich and creamy, then layered with cheese and gravy and baked in the oven. I've tried many versions of polenta over the years, some with wild mushrooms or sun-dried tomatoes, but my favorite is still from my childhood.

Giambotta, a mixture of leftovers, was always tasty. This dish meant different things to different people. My mother's version was peppers, onions and tomatoes cooked and seasoned with eggs set atop to poach. We ate it with crispy bread that was delivered daily to our house. Wine was always on the table, ours for the asking. I preferred my mother's homemade tea, or soda for a rare treat.

Creamy Shrimp Risotto

2 tablespoons olive oil

2 tablespoons butter, melted

1 cup chopped onion

3 cloves garlic, chopped

1⁄4 cup fresh shredded basil leaves

2 cups baby spinach leaves

1 lb. cooked and cleaned shrimp

1⁄2 cup chicken broth

2 cups cooked rice

1⁄2 cup grated Parmesan cheese

Sauté garlic and onion in oil and butter until transparent. Add basil and spinach. Cook until wilted, about 5 minutes. Add shrimp, broth and rice. Sprinkle with cheese.

Don't like to cook rice? Order take-out rice, hot and ready to go, from your local Chinese restaurant. One less thing you have to do.

Classy Crabcakes with Creamy Cocktail Sauce

1 lb. jumbo lump crabmeat

3-4 tablespoons mayonnaise

1 teaspoon Dijon mustard

1 large egg

1 teaspoon horseradish

Dash hot sauce

Dash Worcestershire sauce

1 teaspoon Old Bay seasoning

1 teaspoon lemon juice

Kosher salt and fresh cracked pepper to taste

1 1⁄2 cups fresh bread crumbs

Combine all ingredients except crabmeat and breadcrumbs. Add crabmeat and slowly add fresh breadcrumbs until crab mixture will form patties. Do not over mix. Spray sauté pan with cooking spray and sauté crab cakes until golden, turning once.

Creamy Cocktail Sauce

1 cup mayonnaise

3 tablespoons ketchup

1 tablespoon horseradish

1 teaspoon hot sauce

1⁄4 cup chopped scallions

Combine and chill.

Make fresh breadcrumbs with leftover rolls and sliced bread. Place in food processor and pulse until crumbly. Store in a plastic bag in the freezer. Use for crab cakes, stuffing for mushrooms, etc. It makes a soft and moist filling.

Shrimp and Fagioli

1⁄2 cup olive oil

4 cloves garlic, chopped

Dash hot pepper flakes

2 lbs. cooked and cleaned shrimp

1⁄4 cup chopped Italian flat leaf parsley

1⁄2 cup chicken broth

4 plum tomatoes, diced

1 40-ounce can white beans, drained and rinsed well

Kosher salt and fresh cracked pepper to taste

Sauté garlic and hot pepper flakes in oil. Add shrimp and season with salt, pepper and parsley. Add chicken broth. Cook 5 minutes. Add tomato and beans. Sprinkle with 1⁄2 cup grated Parmesan cheese.

Italian flat leaf parsley will last longer when wrapped in a damp paper towel and stored in the refrigerator. Dampen the paper towel by rinsing the leaves under cold running water and blotting to dry. You can dry the leaves in a salad spinner, too. Store wrapped in a paper towel, not a plastic bag.

Mississippi Sassy Shrimp

4 tablespoons butter, melted
1 1/2 cups chopped onion
1 red pepper, diced
2 stalks celery, diced
4-6 cloves garlic, minced
1 tablespoon Worcestershire sauce
1 tablespoon hot sauce
3 teaspoons Creole seasoning
2 28-ounce cans crushed tomatoes
3 lbs. cooked and cleaned shrimp
2 tablespoons chopped Italian flat leaf parsley
Kosher salt and fresh cracked pepper to taste

Sauté onion, pepper, celery and garlic in butter until fragrant. Add Worcestershire, hot sauce, Creole seasoning and parsley. Cook 5-10 minutes. Add tomatoes and season with salt and pepper. Cook 10-15 minutes, then toss with shrimp. Serve over rice.

Save time and money by buying shrimp that has been cooked, cleaned and frozen. To defrost, cover with cold water and let sit 10-15 minutes.

To cry less when cutting onions, chill onion first, always cut the root end off last and cut by candlelight—the flame burns off the tear-producing gas. Try it. If nothing else, it's romantic!

Pacific Coast Bouillabaisse

6 tablespoons olive oil
2 tablespoons butter, melted
1 1/2 cups chopped onion
6 cloves garlic, chopped
2 bay leaves
1 teaspoon red pepper flakes
3 stalks celery, coarsely chopped
1 cup chopped carrots
2 tablespoons chopped Italian flat leaf parsley
Kosher salt and fresh cracked pepper to taste
1/2 cup white wine
2 cups chunky marinara sauce
1 8-ounce bottle clam juice or 1 cup chicken broth
5 lbs. assorted seafood cut into large chunks (halibut, orange roughy, monk fish, flounder and shrimp.)

Sauté onion, garlic, bay leaves, celery, carrot, red pepper flakes and parsley in oil and butter. Season with salt and pepper. Cook uncovered 10 minutes, stirring frequently. Add white wine, marinara and clam juice. Add assorted seafood. Put in casserole dish and cover. Bake at 350º for 35-40 minutes.

To slice onions evenly and quickly use a Mandolin, a must have tool in the kitchen.

EASY RIDER ON THE OREGON COAST

Clint and I had often talked about a trip like this, and now we had the chance. I had a five-day break in my schedule, so we made plans. Everything was working out perfectly.

We were to fly to Seattle, Washington, pick up a Harley Davidson rental and ride down the coast through Portland and the coast of Oregon to Gold's Beach, then onto the Rogue River. We would take a jet boat ride down Oregon's wild river and then return to Seattle. I planned our stays in beautiful inns along the scenic coast. It wasn't until I contacted the Harley dealer that I realized we were arriving late Saturday night; the dealership would also be closed Sunday and Monday. Fortunately, the rental manager offered a solution. He would deliver the bike to our hotel late Saturday and it would be waiting for us when we arrived. Talk about service! Although it hadn't rained in months and rain was not predicted, the rental manager suggested that we also rent some rain gear.

We arrived in Seattle well after midnight. Our taxi took us to our hotel. There, in the parking lot, was the promised motorcycle—a 2000 Ultra Classic Harley. I had to pack light for our five days of traveling; two saddlebags and a luggage carrier packed with two pair of boots, a leather jacket, helmet, gloves, and vest. Together with Clint's things, we were packed to the gills.

We slept a few hours and then we, well Clint, was up at the crack of dawn. I woke to find him gone, out in the parking lot to try out the bike. Outside it was gray and overcast, not a good sign. Seventy miles into our 300-mile journey, it started to pour. We stopped to put on our rain gear and then drove the rest of the way in the pouring rain. Through highways and winding country roads, it was rain, rain, rain. I don't think it could have rained harder. We had communicators in our helmets enabling us to talk to each other; we laughed through it all.

We arrived at the inn close to 5 p.m., soaked, stiff and tired. Our room had a fireplace and a deck with an incredible view of the Pacific Ocean. As we relaxed we spotted a whale frolicking in the ocean. It was wonderful.

The next morning we started out on our 200-mile ride to our next destination. We rode along the coast enjoying the magnificent view. High winds and no guardrails added to the excitement. It was a bright, sunny day. We were headed to the Winter Spring Ranch, a magnificent 1,000 acre private forest and wildlife preserve tucked away on the southern coast of Oregon. With three guesthouses to choose from, we couldn't go wrong. The beauty and serenity of this remote and pristine ranch proved just what we needed. That night we enjoyed our dinner by the glow of the fireplace and relaxed in the hot tub overlooking the Rogue River. It was a perfect day.

But the drenching rain returned. We had to take cover under a tarp while on our boat trip down the Rogue River. Through the pouring rain we spotted osprey, eagles and a bear.

It took two days to drive the return trip up the coast because of the weather, longer than we had planned. On our way to Seattle to return the motorcycle, we decided to stay a few extra days there just to dry out. Visiting Pike's Market and walking around Puget Sound in the sunshine was the perfect ending to a trip full of challenges and adventure. Good thing Clint and I always pack our sense of humor!

Salmon and Crab Imperial

1 side of salmon—skin removed (approx. 3-3 1/2 lbs.)
1 lb. jumbo lump crabmeat
2 tablespoons butter, melted
1/2 cup chopped onion
1/4 cup chopped scallion
1/2 cup red pepper, chopped
1/2 cup celery, chopped
Kosher salt and fresh cracked pepper to taste
1 tablespoon Creole seasoning
1 teaspoon Dijon mustard
Dash hot sauce
5 tablespoons mayonnaise
1 large egg, beaten
1/4 cup Japanese breadcrumbs
Sprinkle paprika

Sauté onion, scallion, red pepper and celery in melted butter until fragrant, about 5-10 minutes. Season with salt, pepper and Creole seasoning. Add Dijon, hot sauce, 4 tablespoons mayonnaise and crabmeat. Turn off heat and stir in egg. Pour into casserole dish. Top with side of salmon. Rub salmon with remaining tablespoon of mayonnaise. Sprinkle with bread crumbs and paprika. Bake uncovered at 350º for 35-40 minutes.

Scallions are in the onion family. You can use both parts of the scallion. The dark green top is mild while the white bulb has a stronger onion flavor. Store wrapped in a paper towel in the refrigerator. Do not put in a plastic bag.

Crab "Fit for a Queen"

1 lb. jumbo lump crabmeat
1 teaspoon Old Bay seasoning
6 tablespoons mayonnaise
Kosher salt and fresh cracked pepper to taste
1/4 teaspoon cayenne pepper
1 tablespoon Worcestershire sauce
1 cup crushed potato chips
2 teaspoons paprika
4 tablespoons butter, melted

Combine first 6 ingredients and pour into buttered casserole dish. Combine remaining ingredients and pour over crab mixture. Bake uncovered at 350º for 20-25 minutes.

Canned jumbo lump crabmeat has an extended shelf life of four weeks, compared to 2-3 days for crabmeat sold in plastic containers. Both should be stored in the refrigerator.

How Flowers Affect Our Lives

- *Flowers have an immediate impact on happiness.*
- *Flowers make the space in your home more welcoming and create a sharing atmosphere.*

Candlelight is a wondrous thing. I shower by candlelight, pay my bills by candlelight and every night, even if it's just pizza, I eat by candlelight. Put some romance and ambiance in your life with candles. Their glow softens all the edges and makes life (and me) look so much better!

ITALIAN COUNTRYSIDE

GOOD GRAVY

Cooking is my thing, and not just cooking but the whole routine that goes with food. Setting the table with beautiful pottery, candles for ambience, flowers for beauty, ruby red wine swirling in a glass, a wonderful aroma filling the house. Pleasant conversations, some fried hot peppers in oil and garlic cooked to candy-like sweetness on the side. Crunchy, dense bread—broken, not sliced—crumbs scattered on the tablecloth. Creamy sharp cheese glistening with oil, a knife protruding from its wedge. Laughter and shouting, talking about neighbors, friends and celebrations. Black and green olives in oil with flecks of red pepper clinging like confetti. Everyone talking at once, shouting to be heard. This is the feast before the meal.

Steam is pouring out of the pot of water for pasta. It's at a rolling boil before silky strands of pasta are dumped into its cauldron. Meatballs and sausage are submerged in red gravy, bubbling over with great anticipation. A simple salad stands ready as the main meal is served. Grated cheese and pepper flakes are passed as we mound this delicious pasta in our bowls, forks and spoons at the ready. Twist and twirl, the pasta is wrapped tightly around the tines of the fork and disappears quickly as we can't wait to taste the gravy. We dip our bread in the gravy, scooping large chunks into our salivating mouths. We drizzle the gravy with the oil from the hot peppers, then smother fork-tender meatballs in it.

The lifeline of Italian cooking is good gravy, The Secret. Recipes are held dear and passed down from generation to generation with nothing but a whisper, nothing ever written down. Each family member has a trick to make her gravy special, whether it is an onion studded with cloves or a carrot instead of sugar to sweeten the sauce. A variety of meats are a must for a good gravy—meatballs, sausage, pieces of beef, pork, chicken—meticulously browned in olive oil. The famed large, peeled onion, studded with no more than four cloves, a piece of pepper cut in half and seeded, and a half of a peeled carrot, all browned to a carmelized color to add sweetness and flavor to the gravy.

We savor our meal; there is no rush to eat and leave. We remain around the table trying to coax one more meatball into our already too full stomachs. It's too good to rush through; this is a meal to be savored and enjoyed. The noise and conversation happily come along with this meal. It is never fun to eat in silence, and Italians rarely do. As we happily mop up that last bit of carmelized garlic, we swirl the bread around our clean plate saving the extra chunky piece for last. Satisfied and full, we push ourselves up from the table. There is nothing in the world like good gravy!

"Armando's Beef Genovese"

My father tells my mother how to make this dish! (He doesn't cook.)

1 5-6 lb. eye roast
6-8 garlic cloves
Kosher salt and fresh cracked pepper to taste

Marinade

2 cups Chianti wine
1 1/2 cups chopped onion
2 stalks celery, chopped
2 carrots, chopped
2 bay leaves
1 orange rind
1/4 cup olive oil

Make pockets in eye roast with sharp knife. Insert garlic cloves randomly in the roast and season with salt and pepper. Combine marinade ingredients and let meat marinate for approximately 1 hour, turning once. Put meat and marinade in Dutch oven or covered roasting pan and cook at 350º for 2 hours. When cool, remove meat from juices and slice. Take out bay leaves and orange rind and puree marinade in food processor. Heat and serve as gravy for roast.

Gnocchi Alla Romano

I love Gnocchi!

3 cups whole milk ricotta cheese
1 1/2 cups flour
1/2 cup grated Parmesan cheese
1 large egg
Kosher salt to taste
More flour for rolling gnocchi

Combine ricotta, flour, cheese, egg and salt to form dough. Cover with a kitchen towel and let rest for 10-15 minutes. Roll out into logs and cut into 1 inch pieces. Drop into boiling water and cook until they float to the top. Remove with a slotted spoon. Top with your favorite red gravy and grated cheese.

Broccoli Rabe

Bitter broccoli is an acquired taste—once you try it, you'll love it!

2 bunches broccoli rabe, trimmed and rinsed
4 tablespoons olive oil
2 garlic cloves, minced
1 teaspoon red pepper flakes
Kosher salt and fresh cracked pepper to taste
Lemon slices

Trim tough ends off broccoli rabe and discard. Cut broccoli into pieces and rinse well. (Broccoli rabe is sometimes sandy.) Heat oil and cook garlic and red pepper flakes for only a few minutes. You don't want the garlic to get bitter. Add rabe leaves and season with salt and pepper. Stir occasionally. It will cook down tender and delicious. We always serve this with lemon slices.

Seaside Abruzzi Scampi

My father is from Gulianova, a fishing and sea resort town on the Adriatic Coast. When visiting there we always have wonderfully fresh fish!

4-5 lbs. frozen cooked and cleaned shrimp, defrosted and drained well
4 tablespoons butter
4-6 tablespoons olive oil
4-6 cloves garlic, chopped
2 tablespoons chopped Italian flat leaf parsley
2 scallions, chopped
1 teaspoon red pepper flakes
1 tablespoon lemon juice
1/4 cup white wine
Kosher salt and fresh cracked pepper to taste

Sauté garlic, parsley, scallions and red pepper flakes in oil and butter until fragrant. Add remaining ingredients and cook 10-15 minutes. Serve over pasta or by itself with lots of Italian bread for dipping.

Garlic and Oil

Growing up in an Italian household was very special. Until I went to high school I thought everyone was Catholic and Italian. We lived in an all Italian neighborhood. The language was spoken in every corner store, on every porch and at Mass. I grew up eating only Italian food—lucky me! Once I ventured out into the real world I discovered mayonnaise, mustard, ketchup, all sorts of things that were never in my mother's kitchen. Below are a few ways to use GARLIC, OLIVE OIL and SALT & PEPPER. Simple ingredients really, but wonderful and delicious.

- White Pizza Pie: drizzle cooked pizza shell with olive oil, salt and pepper. Cook in oven until warm.
- Hard Boiled Eggs: slice and drizzle with olive oil, salt and pepper. Our Italian "egg salad."
- Cooked Green Beans: toss with olive oil, salt, pepper, garlic and Italian flat leaf parsley. Hot or cold, it's always delicious.
- Fava Beans: shell and serve raw with olive oil, salt, pepper and shaved Parmesan cheese.
- Fennel: a licorice flavor complimented with olive oil, salt and pepper. The fennel is not cooked. Serve raw.
- Italian Potato Salad: cooked potatoes, olive oil, salt, pepper, garlic and Italian flat leaf parsley.
- Toasted Italian Bread: drizzle with olive oil, salt and pepper. Absolutely delicious!
- Tomatoes Sliced with Fresh Basil: drizzle tomatoes with olive oil, salt, pepper and shredded basil. Simple and sweet!

TRACING MY ROOTS

My family is small—half are in Italy. I hear people talk of large family entertaining and all the cousins, aunts and uncles along with grandparents, and I think, we are really only a small group. Small, but powerful comes to mind. Each of us has a very different lifestyle and our own ideas. And we are all vocal and interactive. But all in all, it's fun to be part of this family. My kids hint at dysfunctional but really, everyone I know has encountered some rough water along the way. That's life.

My goal now is to look back upon my relations who crossed the seas, battled the unknown, lived on the land and made my life possible. My roots are Italian; old photos reinforce that my relatives were in the Italian army, sword at their side.

One day I gathered some old photos with my mother and father and we sat down, pen in hand and wrote everyone's name and place in our lineage on the back of the photos. These memories can be too easily lost. I was amazed at the resiliency and strength of my forefathers. Smiles were not on their faces but goodness was in their hearts. And strength—they faced challenges I can't even imagine, but they did it with a zest for life. Enlarged and framed, these photos hang on my walls for inspiration and company as I go through my own life.

Mom's Aglio E Olio

My mother is a fabulous cook. Everything she makes is wonderful. To this day I love to eat at her house. I learned to appreciate good food at her table.

- 1/2 cup olive oil
- 4-8 cloves garlic, chopped
- 1 cup chopped sun-dried tomatoes
- 1 teaspoon hot pepper flakes
- 1 tablespoon chopped Italian flat leaf parsley
- Kosher salt and fresh cracked pepper to taste
- 1/2 cup grated Parmesan cheese
- 1 lb. pasta, cooked (save 1/2 cup pasta water from cooked pasta for sauce)

Cook garlic and tomatoes in oil. Add pepper flakes, parsley and pasta water. Season with salt and pepper. Toss with cooked pasta and top with cheese. Simple and Sensational!

Fried Peppers

The mixture of sweet and sharp flavors, "agro dolce" in Italian, is a wonderful combination.

- 6-8 red or yellow peppers, seeded and cut into strips
- 6 tablespoons olive oil
- 2-4 whole cloves garlic
- 1 anchovy, chopped
- 1 tablespoon brown sugar
- 1 tablespoon balsamic vinegar
- Kosher salt and fresh cracked pepper to taste

Sauté garlic and anchovies in hot oil. Add peppers and cook until softened, about 10 minutes. Add remaining ingredients and cook until balsamic vinegar gets syrupy, about 15-20 minutes. Serve with bread and wine, of course!

Mom's Sausage, Peppers and Potatoes

Another sensational dish from my mother.

3 lbs. sweet Italian sausage, cut into chunks
2 large onions, sliced thin
4 peppers, seeded and cut into chunks
3-4 cloves garlic, smashed
2 lbs. potatoes, cut up
2 tablespoons olive oil

Combine all ingredients and roast covered at 350º for 30 minutes. Uncover and stir well. Roast uncovered for an additional 1 hour or until golden brown.

Homemade sausage from a butcher shop makes this dish even better.

Fabiana's Pasta with Ricotta Cheese and Eggplant

With half of our family living in Italy, we visit each other frequently. This is a recipe from my cousin Fabiana.

4-6 tablespoons olive oil
2-3 cloves garlic, chopped
1 cup chopped onion
1 lb. eggplant, cut into small cubes
1⁄4 cup chopped Italian flat leaf parsley
2 cups marinara sauce
1 cup ricotta cheese
1⁄2 cup grated Parmesan cheese
1 lb. pasta, cooked (reserve 1⁄2 cup of pasta water)

Sauté garlic, onion, eggplant and parsley in hot oil until soft, about 15 minutes. Add marinara, ricotta and pasta water. Cook until creamy and toss with pasta and cheese.

Santina's Gravy

My mother made "gravy" every Saturday morning. I would watch cartoons and smell the wonderful aroma coming from her kitchen. A true Italian gravy has many steps and layers of flavor. It simmered for hours and sat overnight to get more flavorful. Sunday dinner was always homemade fresh pasta and my Mom's delicious gravy meat.

Gravy

1⁄2 cup olive oil
1 large onion (as big as a fist), peel and stud the onion with 3-4 whole cloves (like a Christmas tree ornament!)
1 whole carrot, peeled and cut in half
1 whole pepper, seeded and cut in half
Handful of whole garlic cloves (she sometimes would leave the fine papery thin skin on)
1 29-ounce can crushed tomato
1 29-ounce can tomato puree
1 6-ounce can tomato paste
1 6-ounce can water

Fry onion, carrot, pepper and garlic cloves in oil, turning frequently, for 10-15 minutes. Add remaining ingredients. Simmer on stove for 1 hour, then add browned gravy meat. Cook 1-2 hours more.

Gravy tastes better if it's prepared the day before. When chilled overnight in the refrigerator, the fat that solidifies on the top can be easily removed.

Gravy Meat

1 lb. Italian sausage, cut into pieces and browned
Meatballs (recipe follows)
Bracciole (recipe follows)
1 1⁄4 lb. piece of pork or beef, browned
2-3 pieces chicken, browned

All meat is browned or partially cooked before adding to the gravy. Mom would use a big frying pan and brown the meat on all sides, then set it aside until she made the gravy.

My Mom's Meatballs

When I go to the butcher, I ask for a ground mix of beef, pork and veal. I also tell him to go heavy on the pork because it makes a juicier and tastier meatball.

1 lb. ground mix (beef, pork and veal)
2 medium eggs
2 hard Italian rolls (stale) soaked in water and squeezed dry
Kosher salt and pepper to taste
1/2 cup grated Parmesan cheese
1/4 cup chopped Italian flat leaf parsley
2 cloves garlic, minced
1/2 cup fresh bread crumbs if necessary
Vegetable oil for frying

Mix all of the above ingredients, using the fresh bread crumbs only if the mixture is too wet and won't roll into a ball easily. Heat the skillet before adding the vegetable oil. Heat the oil. Fry the meatballs turning only once. Brown one side thoroughly and then turn once to brown the other side. Remove with slotted spoon. At this point, we would run into the kitchen to eat the meatballs browned and delicious without the gravy. It was a real treat!

STALE Italian bread soaked in water is the key to a softer meatball.

Bracciole

1 lb. bottom round, cut into thin slices for rolling
1/4 lb. proscuitto, sliced thin
2 tablespoons olive oil
1 cup fresh bread crumbs
2 tablespoons chopped Italian flat leaf parsley
1/2 cup grated Parmesan cheese
Kosher salt and fresh cracked pepper to taste
2 cloves garlic, minced

In bowl mix bread crumbs, oil, parsley, cheese, salt, pepper and garlic. Lay meat out flat. Cover surface of meat with sliced proscuitto. Layer with bread crumb mixture. Starting at one end, roll into a log. Tie with butcher string and fry in oil until brown. Set aside to put in gravy.

Other Gravy Meats

Spare ribs or beef ribs, chicken thighs or legs can be used for gravy meat. The greater the variety of meats the tastier the gravy. Just be sure to brown all meats in oil first.

Scripple Soup

These thin crepes take time to make, but are worth the effort. They must be prepared the day they will be served.

6 eggs
3-4 tablespoons grated Parmesan cheese
3-4 tablespoons flour
Kosher salt to taste
1-2 tablespoons water

Combine ingredients and mix until smooth. Spoon a small amount of batter into a HOT, small non-stick sauté pan. Tilt the pan from side to side to evenly spread the mixture and make a very thin crepe. Turn over briefly to cook other side. When cool, roll into logs and cover with chicken broth.

Wine and Fruit

Every year in September my Uncle Funsie made wine in the cellar. The smell of the grapes fermenting spread through the house. We would have his homemade wine with fruit. Strong, potent and sometimes lethal, Uncle Funsie's wine was always a delight to try!

Drunken Strawberries

- 3 cups fresh strawberries, cut up
- 1 cup red wine
- 1⁄4 cup sugar

Mix and enjoy!

Tipsy Peaches

We had three peach trees in our yard so this combination was a natural.

- 1 lb. fresh peaches, cut up
- 1 cup sparkling white wine or red wine
- 1 tablespoon peach schnapps
- Sugar if needed

Combine and let sit for 10 minutes or longer.

Creama Ricotta Con Frutta

A very simple and elegant dessert.

- 2 cups fresh berries (strawberries, blueberries and raspberries)
- 1⁄3 cup sugar
- 2-3 tablespoons hazelnut liqueur
- 3 cups whole milk ricotta cheese
- 3 tablespoons vanilla extract
- 1 cup powdered sugar

Combine berries with sugar and liqueur and set aside. Combine ricotta with vanilla extract and powdered sugar. Spoon into a fancy platter and top with berry mixture.

For a true Sunday Italian dinner, we would start with an antipasto of sharp cheese and soppressata, followed by pasta with gravy with platters of the meat on the side. Next we'd have a green salad and espresso and cakes brought at the bakery after Sunday Mass. It was a true feast, and in this busy world we live in, it's a feast I really miss.

Often, when we have company over, the very first thing out of our mouth is about the mistakes we've made—how we burned something, overcooked it or just plain forgot an ingredient. Don't apologize for anything! Your guests did not read your recipes. If a soufflé falls, call it a flan.

Frame a favorite recipe written in your mother's or aunt's hand. Hang it in your kitchen.

Change is often difficult. We feel familiar with our problems and pain. It is hard to let go and start new. Make a list of the things that you would like to change in your life. Take one issue at a time. Write it down. Ask yourself for direction and help. You, in your own heart, know what is best for you.

SIDE DISHES

Florentine White Beans and Spinach

3 cloves garlic, minced

4 tablespoons olive oil

1 teaspoon hot pepper flakes

1 1⁄2 lbs. spinach leaves, rinsed well

1 40-ounce can white beans, drained and rinsed

1⁄2 cup grated Parmesan cheese

Kosher salt and fresh cracked pepper to taste

Sauté garlic in hot oil with hot pepper flakes. Add spinach and cook until wilted. Add beans and cook 10-15 minutes stirring occasionally. Season with salt and pepper

Santina's Baked Squash

2 tablespoons olive oil

2 tablespoons butter

2-3 cloves garlic, minced

2-3 onions, sliced thin (about 4 cups)

3 zucchini, cut up (about 4 cups)

4 eggs beaten

Kosher salt and fresh cracked pepper to taste

1⁄2 teaspoon dried thyme

1 cup grated Parmesan cheese (plus additional 1/4 cup for topping)

Cook the onions and garlic in butter and oil until translucent. Add zucchini and cook until soft. This cooking process will render a lot of juice. Drain and reserve this juice and add it to 4 beaten eggs, salt, pepper, thyme and Parmesan cheese. In an ovenproof pottery dish, layer the onion, garlic and zucchini. Top with egg mixture and 1⁄4 cup additional cheese. Bake uncovered at 350º for 35-40 minutes or until golden.

When making a dish ahead of time, cook it for half the recommended bake time. Then cool and refrigerate. To reheat, always bring food to room temperature first, then cook for remaining time in the oven or until hot.

Mediterranean Bean and Vegetable Stew

Serve with crusty bread and wine!

1 large eggplant (1 lb.), cubed with skin on

4-6 tablespoons olive oil

2 stalks celery, chopped

1 1⁄2 cups chopped onion

2-3 cloves garlic, chopped

1 red pepper, seeded and chopped

4 tablespoons chopped fresh basil

1 zucchini, cubed

2 cups marinara sauce

3 tablespoons honey

1 40-ounce can white beans, drained and rinsed

Sauté eggplant in oil until browned. Remove from pan. Add more oil to the pan if necessary and sauté onion, celery, garlic, red pepper, basil and zucchini. Cook until fragrant and browned, about 15 minutes. Add cooked eggplant, marinara, honey and beans. Pour in an ovenproof dish and cover. Bake at 350º for 30-35 minutes.

When choosing an eggplant, look for a dark, shiny skin with no blemishes or soft parts. It is not necessary to peel an eggplant.

When cooking eggplant, be sure the oil in the sauté pan is hot. When hot, add eggplant and stir frequently. If the eggplant absorbs all of the oil, add 1-2 tablespoons water and continue cooking. The eggplant will eventually release the oil as it cooks.

Baked Tomatoes Provencal

1 lb. grape tomatoes, stems removed and rinsed
1/4 cup shredded basil
Kosher salt and fresh cracked pepper to taste
6 tablespoons olive oil
3 cloves garlic, minced
1 1/2 cups fresh bread crumbs
1/4 cup grated Parmesan cheese

Sauté garlic and basil lightly in oil for 5 minutes. Add bread crumbs and toss with tomatoes. Pour into ovenproof pottery dish and top with cheese. Bake uncovered at 350º for 20-25 minutes.

Roasted Winter Vegetables

3 carrots, peeled and cut into 1 inch pieces
2 leeks, rinsed and chopped
1 lb. brussel sprouts, trimmed and cut in half
1 sweet potato, peeled and cubed
2 peppers, seeded and cut into strips
6 tablespoons olive oil
1 1/2 cups chicken broth
1 teaspoon dried thyme
Kosher salt and fresh cracked pepper to taste
1 cup corn kernels (fresh, frozen or canned, drained)
2 tablespoons chopped Italian flat leaf parsley

Combine all ingredients. Roast covered at 350º for 30 minutes. Uncover and stir vegetables. Roast uncovered at 350º for an additional 30 minutes.

To trim brussel sprouts, cut off a piece at the root end. The tough outer leaves will fall away.

To clean oven spills, sprinkle the area with salt immediately. When the oven has cooled, clean with a damp cloth.

A PERFECT WEDDING IN MAY

Sunny skies above, a calm, happy bride peers out an upstairs window at the beautiful grounds below. The dashing groom, beaming from ear to ear, is happily greeting guests as the valet service whisks their cars to the parking area. The planning, preparation and work are behind them (catering your own wedding is an awesome task), the fun and celebration about to begin.

The immaculately white, 40' x 80' tent shimmers in the sun. Inside the tent, 500 yards of netting is draped from pole to pole. Thousands of twinkling lights glitter like stars in the Milky Way. Two hundred and fifty feet of ivy grace the poles. Glass candle chandeliers filled with fresh flowers hang from the center of the tent. Thirty-five round tables with bowls of fresh wildflowers surrounded by votive candles are scattered throughout. Hundreds of luminaries line the pathways waiting to be lit at dusk.

The band leader belts out Sinatra and Tony Bennett tunes as the guests arrive. Hors d'oeuvres are being prepared in the 20' x 20' cooking tent. Under the arbor of wisteria, the mayor awaits the bride. Themes from "The Godfather" float through the air, radiating from a mandolin played by the bride's brother.

The ceremony, scheduled to begin at three o'clock, is a little delayed. A train has pulled into the station next door and must depart before the ceremony can start. The train finally pulls away; the ceremony begins. The bride's parents, the father dressed in a tux complete with 'Godfather' hat and gloves, accompany their daughter down the aisle to the smiling groom. Happiness can't be contained and smiles and tears are in everyone's eyes. The ceremony is short and sweet. The only interruptions are from the bride, unable to keep from kissing the groom throughout the ceremony. Vows are exchanged. Let the party begin!

Under the tent a raw bar, sushi table, cold seafood table, and hot and cold hors d'oeuvres tables present a multitude of some 30 different delectable appetizers.

A five-piece band provides the dinner entertainment. At seven o'clock, the 32-foot buffet is unveiled. The antipasto bar alone has more than 15 different kinds of salads, vegetables and breads. Eight different pasta dishes and meat entrees line the way to a 200 lb. roast pig.

During dinner, a friend of the couple plays the blues on his guitar and the bride's uncle plays the Italian accordion. At 8:30, the D.J. starts the dance music and everyone jams under the candlelit tent and in the garden.

A gorgeous wedding cake with fondant icing and pink ribbons highlights the 24-foot sweet table. Coffee, tea, an assortment of mints and chocolates, and liquors from the full service bar bring a close to a magical wedding day.

Effortless Food Preparation

- Read your recipes all the way through.
- Gather your ingredients, utensils and dishes.
- Clean as you go.
- Cook in beautiful ovenproof pottery that can go from oven to table.

"Christmas" Peas

Not only for Christmas, this dish gets its name from the vibrant Christmas colors.

1 1/2 cups chopped onion
2 red peppers, seeded and diced
3-4 tablespoons olive oil
2-3 cloves garlic, minced
6 cups frozen peas, defrosted
Kosher salt and fresh cracked pepper to taste

Sauté garlic, onion and peppers in hot oil until carmelized,10-15 minutes. Season with salt and pepper. Add peas and cook additional 15-20 minutes.

Bistro Carrots

1/2 cup olive oil
1 tablespoon Dijon mustard
1 tablespoon lemon juice
1 tablespoon honey
Kosher salt and fresh cracked pepper to taste
1 1/2 lbs. carrots, peeled and cut into disks
1/3 cup chopped Italian flat leaf parsley
5 scallions, chopped

In sauté pan, whisk together oil, Dijon, lemon juice and honey. Add salt, pepper, parsley and scallion. Cook 5 minutes. Cook carrots in boiling water until tender. Drain and toss hot carrots with olive oil mixture.

Sun-Kissed Carrots

2 16-ounce bags baby carrots, cooked until tender
3 tablespoons butter
1 tablespoon honey
1 tablespoon orange marmalade
1 tablespoon triple sec
Kosher salt and fresh cracked pepper to taste
1 teaspoon dried tarragon

Combine all ingredients in saucepan and toss with carrots.

You can experiment with different jams and preserves. Try using apricot or peach preserves instead of marmalade.

Asparagus with Carmelized Garlic

2 lbs. asparagus spears, trimmed and cooked until tender
1/3 cup whole garlic cloves
1/3 cup olive oil
Kosher salt and fresh cracked pepper to taste

In sauté pan, cook garlic in olive oil with salt and pepper until garlic turns golden and soft. (You will be able to smash it with a wooden spoon. This takes about 20-25 minutes.) Pour over cooked asparagus. Can be made ahead and reheated.

It's important to have the right tools in your kitchen. More important is to have them where you can easily access them—not in the back of a cabinet or behind five layers of pots and pans, where you'll never find them. Keep your kitchen stocked and ready to go. It makes it so much more fun to cook!

Creamy Asparagus

2 lbs. asparagus cut up into 1 inch pieces, rinsed well (reserve 1 cup asparagus water)

4 tablespoons flour

4 tablespoons butter

1 cup heavy cream

Pinch paprika

Kosher salt and fresh cracked pepper to taste

4 hard boiled eggs, chopped

Topping

1 cup coarsely chopped buttery crackers

1 cup fresh bread crumbs

4 tablespoons butter, melted

1⁄2 cup grated Parmesan cheese

Cook asparagus and drain, reserving 1 cup of the cooking liquid for recipe. Melt butter and add flour. Cook until golden. Whisk in 1 cup asparagus cooking liquid and 1 cup heavy cream. Season with salt and pepper. In an ovenproof pottery dish, layer cooked asparagus, hard boiled eggs and cream sauce. Repeat if necessary. Combine ingredients for topping and spread evenly over asparagus. Bake uncovered at 350º for 25-30 minutes.

When making a béchamel or cream sauce, cook equal parts of flour and butter until it is a golden paste. Warm the milk before adding to the roux. This will prevent lumps and it will get smooth and creamy very easily. Milk can be warmed in a glass measuring cup in the microwave.

Asparagus with Raspberry Vinaigrette

Colorful and Different!

2 lbs. asparagus, trimmed and cooked until tender (5-10 minutes depending on the thickness of stalks)

Cool asparagus.

Raspberry Vinaigrette

1⁄2 cup olive oil

2 cloves garlic

1 tablespoon Dijon mustard

1 tablespoon honey

1 tablespoon red wine vinegar

1 tablespoon raspberry preserves

Kosher salt and fresh cracked pepper to taste

1⁄2 cup fresh raspberries.

Combine vinaigrette ingredients in a food processor and pour over asparagus just before serving. Garnish with 1 cup fresh raspberries. Serve at room temperature.

Asparagus Parmesan

3 lbs. asparagus, cooked 5-10 minutes or until tender

6 tablespoons butter, melted

3⁄4 cup grated Parmesan cheese

Fresh cracked pepper to taste

Layer asparagus in ovenproof pottery dish. Drizzle with butter and sprinkle with Parmesan cheese. Bake uncovered at 350º for 20-25 minutes.

ANTIQUING IN ITALY

It's the middle of winter. Cold air fills the January sky. It may seem like an unlikely time to visit Italy, but I'll let you in on a secret—it's the best time to go. We are frequent travelers to Europe in the winter months. Low airfare, and uncrowded hotels and restaurants bring us back again and again.

We are on a 10-day trip with my parents. Our base is a former Italian villa, now a charming pensione, complete with on-site parking (quite unusual in Italy) near the Arno River in Florence. We take walks through small neighborhoods, passing wonderfully tiny antique shops filled with ancient artifacts of European history. We inhale the enticing aromas of carcofi and garlic roasted meats seeping out from shuttered restaurant doorways posted with handwritten signs announcing the daily specials.

We watch the people, so elegant and stylish, as they stop to talk with their neighbors, kissing cheeks and sharing passionate conversation in the warmth of the Italian sunshine. A quick espresso is downed in half the time it takes the huge espresso machine to hiss and squirt it into the tiny cup. This is Italy, the place I love, where I feel I belong.

As Sunday morning church bells echo through the city, we are off to Arezzo, a quaint hill town tucked into the Tuscan countryside. It seems as if everyone is headed to the biggest antique show in the land. Compact Italian cars cruise through the winding streets, looking for a parking space amidst the multitudes of families, flower vendors and churchgoers. Mothers and daughters walk arm in arm. The men stroll behind, hands clasped behind their backs, surveying the scenes around them.

On this winter day the sunshine is brilliant, the sky a cornflower blue. We climb the steep steps up the piazza and walk through the archway of the city into its bustling center. I am totally unprepared for the scene that awaits. There, amidst ancient walls, historic frescoes and massive columns, are tables upon tables filled with bits of history. (Antiques take on a new meaning in Europe. What we consider old in America is a baby by comparison.) We are surrounded by armor, carved sleigh beds, old gladiator's helmets, clothing and costumes from centuries ago. My eyes dart everywhere, taking it all in. With lire stashed in my pockets and a time set to meet for lunch, I set off to see what treasures I can find to stuff into my suitcase.

Chinese slippers, silver place settings, antique lace, old and stately furniture, church benches, confessionals, cherubs, holy statues, and rich brocade fabric fill the stalls. It's truly beyond my wildest dreams. The piazza gives way to narrow alleys filled with people strolling and eating gelato. Church bells ring to announce the hour. Here you don't have to look at your watch; just listen and you'll know the time.

The air is fragrant with the preparation of lunch, a big meal in Italy, especially on Sunday. Families linger for hours over al dente pasta and roasted meats. Wine bottles stand proud, lining the tables like centerpieces of a gourmet meal. Even the children know the routine. They take lunch seriously, just like their parents.

We eat in a local restaurant. We are the only tourists. It's just as I like it, the regional foods, flavors of the land, set amidst a passionate and talkative crowd. We eat and drink with gusto, just as my ancestors did before me.

Spinach with Raisins and Pine Nuts

3 tablespoons olive oil
2 tablespoons butter, melted
1/2 cup golden raisins
4 ounces pine nuts
Kosher salt and fresh cracked pepper to taste
3 lbs. spinach, washed

Sauté spinach in hot oil with salt and pepper until wilted. Drain any excess liquid. In a separate sauté pan, cook the pine nuts and raisins in butter. Toss with spinach.

Spinach and Potatoes with Garlic

4-5 tablespoons olive oil
2-3 cloves garlic, chopped
2 lbs. spinach, washed
1 cup cooked potatoes, cubed
Kosher salt and fresh cracked pepper to taste

Sauté garlic in hot oil, add spinach and cook until wilted. Add cooked potatoes and season with salt and pepper.

Green Beans with Pine Nuts and Basil

You can substitute almonds, hazelnuts or walnuts for the pine nuts in this recipe.

2 lbs. green beans, trimmed and blanched
3-4 tablespoons olive oil
3 cloves garlic, minced
1/4 cup pine nuts
2 tablespoons chopped fresh basil
Kosher salt and fresh cracked pepper to taste

Sauté garlic in oil until fragrant. Add pine nuts and basil. Add green beans. Season with salt and pepper and cook 5-10 minutes more.

Broccoli with Parmesan Garlic Crumbs

2 bunches broccoli, cut up and cooked until tender
4 tablespoons olive oil
2 cloves garlic, chopped
1 cup fresh bread crumbs
1/2 cup grated Parmesan cheese
Kosher salt and fresh cracked pepper to taste

Cook garlic in oil. Add bread crumbs, cheese, salt and pepper. Toss with broccoli.

Green Beans with Garlic Hazelnut Aioli

3 lbs. green beans, trimmed and cooked until tender
1 tablespoon Dijon mustard
2 cloves garlic
3/4 cup olive oil
Kosher salt and fresh cracked pepper to taste
1/2 cup grated Parmesan cheese
1 tablespoon lemon juice
1 tablespoon hazelnut oil

Combine all ingredients except green beans in a food processor. Toss aioli with warm green beans.

Maple Mashed Sweet Potatoes

2 40-ounce cans sweet potatoes, drained
5 tablespoons butter, melted
1/2 cup maple syrup
Kosher salt and fresh cracked pepper to taste

Combine butter with syrup. Add potatoes and smash with a wooden spoon. Season with salt and pepper. Bake covered at 350º for 20-25 minutes.

Cheesy Broccoli Soufflé

2 heads broccoli, cut up and cooked 5-10 minutes
1 10-ounce can cream of celery soup
1 cup mayonnaise
2 eggs
1 cup shredded cheddar cheese
1⁄2 cup grated Parmesan cheese

Topping

1 cup homemade bread crumbs
1⁄2 cup grated Parmesan cheese
4 tablespoons butter, melted

Mix together cream of celery soup, mayonnaise, eggs, cheddar and Parmesan cheeses. Combine with cooked broccoli. Pour into ovenproof pottery dish. Combine ingredients for topping and sprinkle on top of broccoli. Bake uncovered at 350º for 30-35 minutes.

Chili Roasted Potatoes

2 tablespoons butter, melted
3 tablespoons olive oil
1 1⁄2 cups chopped onion
1 red pepper, seeded and diced
4 cloves garlic, chopped
1 tablespoon Worcestershire sauce
1 tablespoon Creole seasoning
Dash hot sauce
3 lbs. red bliss potatoes, cut up and cooked in unsalted water, 5-7 minutes, drained

Cook all ingredients except potatoes in oil, stirring until combined and fragrant, 10-15 minutes. Toss with potatoes. Pour into an ovenproof pottery dish. Roast uncovered at 350º for 30-35 minutes.

Creamy Onions

1 10-ounce can cream of chicken soup
1 1⁄2 cups half & half
1 tablespoon soy sauce
Fresh cracked pepper to taste
2 large onions, sliced (about 3 cups)
2-3 tablespoons butter, melted
2 cups shredded Swiss cheese
8-10 slices of Italian bread (cut from a roll) buttered on one side
1 teaspoon paprika

Combine soup, half & half, soy sauce and pepper. Set aside. Melt butter in sauté pan. Cook sliced onions until translucent. (Cover onions for first 5 minutes to sweat them.) Combine cooked onions with cheese and soup mixture. Pour into ovenproof pottery dish. Layer buttered bread slices on top. Sprinkle with paprika. Bake uncovered at 350º for 25-30 minutes.

To "sweat onions" means to cook them over high heat, covered so that they release their juices and flavors. This takes about 10 minutes. To carmelize them, uncover and continue cooking until they turn golden brown in color. This will take an additional 10-15 minutes.

Baked Macaroni and Blue Cheese

3 tablespoons butter, melted
3 tablespoons flour
2 cups whole milk
1 cup heavy cream
2 cups shredded white cheddar cheese
1 cup crumbled blue cheese
Kosher salt and fresh cracked pepper to taste
1 lb. elbow pasta, cooked and drained

Topping

1 cup homemade bread crumbs
1⁄2 cup butter, melted
1⁄2 cup crumbled blue cheese

Warm whole milk and heavy cream. In sauté pan, combine butter and flour. Cook until it forms a golden paste, 5-10 minutes. Slowly whisk in milk and cream. Cook until thick. Add cheese, season with salt and pepper and toss with pasta. Pour into an ovenproof pottery dish. Combine ingredients for topping and sprinkle on pasta. Bake uncovered at 350º for 25-30 minutes.

Smashed Potatoes with Cheddar and Bacon

3 lbs. potatoes
1 cup shredded cheddar cheese
6 slices bacon, cut up and cooked until crisp; drain
1 cup half & half
6 tablespoons butter
Kosher salt and fresh cracked pepper to taste

Cook potatoes in salted water until very tender. Rinse and drain. Combine ingredients while potatoes are still hot. Add butter FIRST, then cheese, half & half, salt and pepper. Add bacon last.

Can be made ahead and reheated. If it is too thick add more half & half until creamy. It's OK for potatoes to be lumpy. This is called "smashed" potatoes—NOT "mashed!"

Put some "zing" in your mashed potatoes.

Try adding one of these.

- grated cheddar or Swiss cheese
- crumbled feta cheese
- chopped pimento stuffed olives
- olive oil instead of butter
- horseradish
- carmelized onions or garlic
- pesto
- crumbled blue cheese

Sweet Potato Soufflé

2 40-ounce cans sweet potatoes or yams, drained
1⁄2 cup brown sugar
1⁄2 teaspoon nutmeg
1⁄2 teaspoon cinnamon
Kosher salt to taste
4 large eggs, beaten
1 cup heavy cream

Drain sweet potatoes and mash. Combine remaining ingredients. Pour into ovenproof pottery dish. Sprinkle with topping.

Topping

4 tablespoons butter, melted
4 tablespoons flour
4 tablespoons brown sugar

Combine ingredients until crumbly. Top sweet potatoes and bake uncovered at 350º for 45-50 minutes or until set.

Follow your intuition. How many times has that little voice inside of you begged to be heard but you just brushed it aside? Go with the flow. Listen to that voice. It's usually right!

If you don't make mistakes in your life, it's probably because you are not taking chances. The more mistakes we make, the more we will grow and succeed—especially when we learn from our mistakes.

It's never too late to go on an adventure. Learning something new can be exciting and fun. Take an Italian class, learn to water color, do that something you always wished you had time for. Remember, life is not a dress rehearsal. It's now or never.

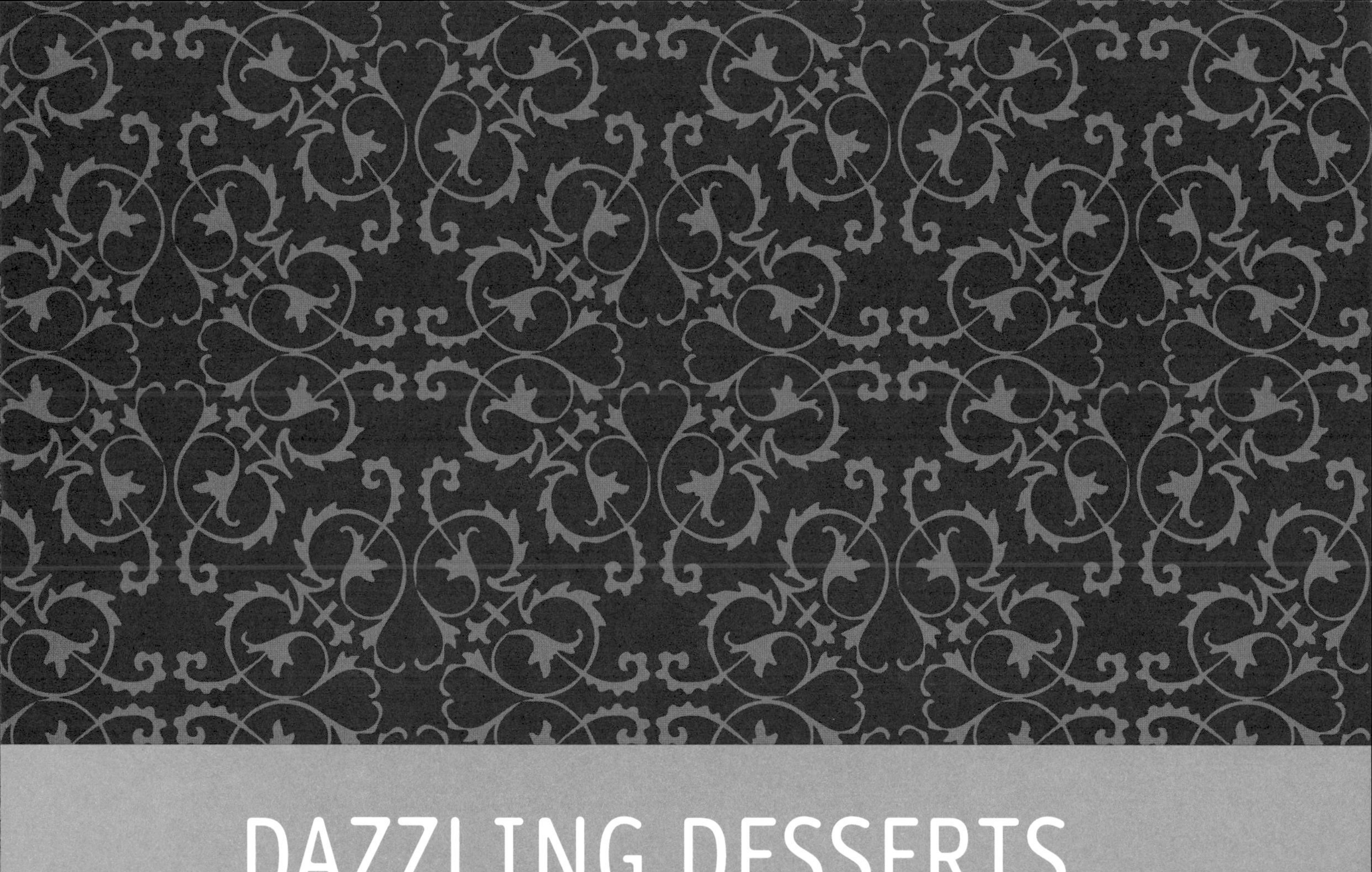

DAZZLING DESSERTS

Vanilla Extract

Make your own vanilla extract with 6-8 vanilla beans cut in half. Put them in a pint jar and cover them with vodka. Keep in a cool dark place for 4-6 weeks and you will have a wonderful vanilla extract.

I always keep two jars of vanilla extract in my cabinet. When one gets low, I refill it with vodka and let it sit another few weeks. I never have to discard the beans. Every once in a while add 2 or 3 more beans and you have vanilla for life. I am leaving my children one jar each in my will!

Cinnamon Bun Bread Pudding

- 2 cups half & half
- 2 cups heavy cream
- 8 large eggs, beaten
- 1 cup sugar
- 2 teaspoons vanilla extract
- 1 teaspoon nutmeg
- 1 teaspoon cinnamon
- 2 lbs. cinnamon buns

Combine first 7 ingredients. Tear cinnamon buns into pieces and layer in a pretty ovenproof pottery dish. Pour mixture over buns and let sit for 20 minutes to allow the cinnamon buns to absorb the custardy mixture. Bake covered at 350º for 35-45 minutes or until it smells so good you can't stand it!

My Favorite Rice Pudding

- 4 cups rice
- 2 2/3 cups sugar
- 2 sticks butter (1/2 lb.)
- 3 quarts milk
- 1 quart light cream

Boil 8 cups water in a big pot. Add the rice and cook for 5 minutes, stirring occasionally. Drain the rice and put it back into the pot. Add the sugar and butter and cook over low heat until butter melts. Add milk and light cream. Simmer, stirring occasionally, until liquid is absorbed, about 30 minutes.

Italian Rice Pie

This is an Italian holiday treat.

- 3 lbs. whole milk ricotta cheese
- 1 quart light cream
- 12 eggs
- 2 cups sugar
- 2 tablespoons vanilla extract
- 2 cups cooked rice

Whisk the ricotta with eggs, cream, sugar and vanilla. Stir in rice. Pour into ovenproof pottery dish. Bake uncovered at 350º for 1-1 1/2 hours or until set. Cool (if you can wait that long) and serve.

Dolci Fragole "Sweet Strawberries"

As a dessert for a sit down dinner, I put 2-3 tablespoons of this sauce on a pretty cake dish, top with sliced fresh strawberries and serve with fresh whipped cream. You'll think you're in heaven! It's also a wonderful sauce for dipping strawberries.

- 1/2 cup heavy cream
- 8 ounces cream cheese, softened
- 4 tablespoons brown sugar
- 2 tablespoons frangelica
- 2 tablespoons amaretto
- 2 tablespoons triple sec

Combine all ingredients in food processor. Serve with giant strawberries.

To sanitize your kitchen sponge, microwave it on high until it's too hot to touch.

Raspberry Gratin

- 3 cups fresh raspberries
- 2 tablespoons sugar
- 2 tablespoons triple sec
- 3 eggs
- 1/2 cup sugar
- 1/2 cup flour
- Pinch salt

Toss together raspberries, sugar and triple sec in ovenproof pottery or 9 inch pie dish. Beat together the remaining ingredients and pour mixture on top of raspberries. Sprinkle with 2 tablespoons of sugar. Bake uncovered at 350º for 20-25 minutes.

GOING TO THE BAKERY

Sunday mornings after church we would pile into the back of my father's car. We were sometimes allowed to bring a friend, so we crammed back there four or five strong. It was a time before seat belts, and, those of us lucky enough to have called a window seat, hung our heads out of the car. We were headed for the bakery, my reward for sitting through Sunday Mass.

My dad parked the car on 63rd Street to stay out of the way of the trolley tracks that crisscrossed the street. We walked the couple of blocks to the local Italian bakery, knowing there would be a line when we got there. There was always a line at the bakery. We took a paper number and spent the next few minutes with our noses pressed to the glass cases dreaming of what we would order. The cases were filled with cookies, St. Joseph cakes, rum cakes, pineapple ricotta pies and my favorite, sugar jelly donuts. Crisp cannoli shells were waiting to be filled with creamy ricotta filling studded with pieces of chocolate. The ladies who worked there wore white nylon uniforms, a cross between a nurse and a waitress. There was an equal number of mean and nice ladies, so it was the luck of the draw to get a nice, smiling one sure to hand over a cookie to enjoy before pointing out our choices.

The ladies went from case to case with boxes and tiny pieces of wax paper in hand, plucking the sweets as you pointed them out. They would fill the box, then sprinkle everything with powdered white or granulated sugar for extra goodness. If you ordered cookies, a handful of white-coated almonds called confetti were thrown over top for decoration. These ladies expertly closed and tied the boxes together with string that came from a bountiful source somewhere under the counter, as if they'd been doing it all their lives.

Packages in hand, we headed back to the car, thinking of ways we could coax a donut out of our mother before our big Sunday meal. Our anticipation grew for the sweets nestled in the box in the corner of the kitchen, set next to the espresso pot packed with strong coffee. After a meal that sometimes lasted three or four hours, we were finally allowed to grab that donut and take it outside, sugar spilling down our chins and onto our shirts, licking sticky hands, trying to capture all that sugar.

Another Sunday passes and the anticipation begins for the next week's trip to the bakery.

Snazzy Brownies with Delectable Sauces

Make your favorite brownies and serve with one or more of these delicious sauces. Don't forget the ice cream!

Irish Cream Sauce

2 cups semi-sweet chocolate chips

1 1⁄2 cups heavy cream

1⁄2 cup Irish cream liqueur

Melt chocolate in saucepan and whisk in cream and liqueur.

Chocolate Liqueur Sauce

2 cups heavy cream

1 tablespoon chocolate syrup

2 tablespoons chocolate liqueur

1⁄2 cup powdered sugar

Combine ingredients in food processor until thick; it will look like a chocolate whipped cream.

Raspberry Sauce

1 16-ounce bag frozen raspberries, defrosted and drained

1⁄2 cup sugar

1⁄4 cup triple sec

Combine ingredients in saucepan and heat for 5-10 minutes. Chill and serve.

Cannoli Cake

2 lbs. whole milk ricotta cheese

1 1⁄2 cups powdered sugar

1 tablespoon vanilla extract

1⁄4 cup crème de cocoa

1⁄4 cup mini chocolate chips

2-3 dozen lady fingers

1⁄4 cup crème de cocoa or amaretto to sprinkle on lady fingers as layering

Whip together ricotta, sugar, vanilla extract and crème de cocoa. Blend in chocolate chips. In a glass bowl, layer 1/3 lady fingers and drizzle with crème de cocoa or amaretto. Add 1/3 ricotta mixture and repeat steps until finished.

Topping

2 cups heavy cream

1⁄2 cup powdered sugar

1 tablespoon vanilla pudding mix

Combine topping ingredients in food processor until whipped. Scoop on top of layered lady fingers.

A food processor is a great way to whip cream in a flash!

Peanut Butter Cup Mousse

A great way to use left over peanut butter cups from Halloween!

- 4 8-ounce packs cream cheese, softened
- 2 cups sugar
- 2 cups peanut butter
- 2 cups heavy cream
- 3 tablespoons vanilla extract
- 4 tablespoons powdered sugar
- 5 packs peanut butter cups, chopped

In food processor combine cream cheese, sugar and peanut butter. (You may have to do this in batches.) Remove mixture from processor and set aside in large mixing bowl. Combine heavy cream, vanilla extract and powered sugar in same processor bowl. Mix until light and fluffy, about 5 minutes. Fold into cream cheese mix along with chopped pieces of peanut butter cups. Swirl glaze on top and spoon into a pretty bowl. Chill and serve.

Glaze

- 6 ounces chocolate chips
- 6 ounces heavy cream

Melt and whisk together over low heat.

Krispy Kreme Bread Pudding

Believe it or not, this is not a "really sweet" dessert but it's very delicious!

- 8 large eggs
- 3 cups half & half
- 1 cup heavy cream
- 1 teaspoon vanilla extract
- 2 dozen Krispy Kreme glazed doughnuts, cut up

Place doughnuts in an ovenproof pottery dish. Whisk remaining ingredients together and pour over doughnuts. Let sit for 20 minutes to allow doughnuts to absorb some of the liquid. Bake covered at 350º for 45-50 minutes or until set.

CICERCHIATTA "Honey Balls"

Hard to pronounce but easy to make, these little sweets are a treat during the holidays.

- 2 1/2 cups flour
- 1/3 cup sugar
- 3 eggs
- 1/4 cup olive oil
- 2 tablespoons triple sec

Combine flour and sugar in food processor. Add remaining ingredients. Process until the dough comes together. Remove and cover with a kitchen towel. Let dough rest for 10-15 minutes, then roll into little balls. Fry in 1-1 1/2 cups vegetable oil. "Honey Balls" will puff up while frying. Drain on paper towels and toss with honey mixture.

Honey Mixture

- 1 cup honey
- 2 tablespoons sugar

Combine in saucepan over low heat until sugar melts. Garnish with 1/2 cup sliced almonds and multi-colored sprinkles.

Brandy Bread Pudding

- 2 loaves cinnamon bread
- 8 tablespoons butter, cut up
- 1 1/2 cups brown sugar
- 1/2 cup brandy
- 4 cups light cream
- 8 eggs

Mix eggs with light cream and brandy. Layer bread with butter and brown sugar. Repeat if necessary. Pour cream and egg mixture on top. Let sit 10-15 minutes until liquid is absorbed. Bake covered at 350º for 45-55 minutes. Serve with vanilla sauce.

Vanilla Sauce

- 1 5.1-ounce box instant vanilla pudding
- 1 cup milk
- 1 1/2 cups heavy cream
- 1/2 cup brandy

Whisk together until thick. Serve cold.

DRIVE IT LIKE YOU STOLE IT

My preparation started 18 months earlier. I traded in my automatic car for a stick shift. I had an ulterior motive. In order to drive a NASCAR racecar, I needed to be able to shift gears. It was a dream of mine for a while, a goal I'd set, an experience I wanted. After some frustration and much laughter, I learned how to maneuver my little stick shift car. A much hinted for birthday gift of a 1-800-BE-PETTY racing experience was mine at last! Clint, with a gleam in his eye, would be going, too. We were in this together.

The first available date was Tuesday, June 24, at noon. We couldn't wait. Clint, who has more driving experience than I, especially with driving stick shift, was a shoe-in. No way was I going to beat him. His shifting is as smooth as lightening; he is Harry Gant and Dale Earnhardt all rolled into one. I listened to everything he told me, took any hint I could, knowing I was up against what Darrell Waltrip calls "sperience."

I tried to anticipate the feeling of this experience, yet knew my imagination was coming up short. Driving 80 m.p.h. down I-95 is nothing compared to driving a NASCAR racecar with a 600-horsepower engine at 150 m.p.h. on a one-and-a-half-mile, banked racetrack. There's just no comparison.

Since I'd already talked about this opportunity so excitedly to everyone and anyone, there was no way I could back out. No matter how nervous I became, I had to go through with it. And boy was I getting nervous.

It's all anticipation, adrenaline, excitement and butterflies as we enter the infield at Lowe's Motor Speedway in North Carolina this sunny, hot June morning. We are greeted by the roar of a powerful engine, at first whining in the distance, then coming closer into turn three and rocketing through turn four into the front stretch. We see two cars, close together, roaring around the track. "Oh my God, that's going to be us!" I am sweating and I know it's not just the North Carolina sun. What had I gotten myself into?

As we arrive at the media center meeting place I notice the fire trucks, EMTs and safety crews. All at once, it hits me that this is the "real deal." We hand over multiple medical forms and releases, each with a signature acknowledging that we are responsible for anything that might happen. We sign our life away to drive a racecar.

We put on our Petty blue racing suits. Looking like real racecar drivers, we head out to the track. The 22 men and two women are divided into four groups. Clint and I are assigned to separate groups. We will race two sets, eight laps in the first set, 10 laps in the second. We are instructed to go fast and to stay as close as possible to the pace car. The instructors will give us feedback after the first set. They quickly explain how to climb into and out of the car through the window, what to do if a tire goes flat, where the fire extinguisher is located in case the motor blows up, and, if necessary, how to get out of the safety gear and out of the car in a hurry.

Clint goes first, driving Dale Jarrett's UPS #88 car. Strapped in by his pit crew, he is off like a rocket down pit road onto the track. Around and around, it's just a matter of minutes before he rips back into pit road and slides out of the car. With fire in his eyes and hands shaking, Clint rushes over to tell me to "grab hold of that wheel, give the gas all you got, concentrate on the car in front of you, and oh, remember to have a

(Continued on next page>>)

great time!" The best advice in the world from my very own, real life crew chief. I am ready!

My instructor motions for me. It's MY turn. One foot first and then the other, I bend my body into the car and slide into the seat. The crew adjusts my helmet and straps me in tight. As he puts up the window net, the instructor tells me to, "Drive it like you stole it!" He flips the ignition switch and I am off and out of the pits at 130 m.p.h., the back of the pace car burning in my view. I take turn one up on the apron of the track. Into turn two, I drive close to the wall, too close. Here comes turn three, 'go into it hard, against your instincts.' I ricochet out of turn four and onto the front stretch. I am driving a racecar at 150 m.p.h. The car is set up perfect, sticking to the track like glue yet it feels as if I'm gliding around the track. The smell of rubber fills the air; the roar of the throttle is music to my ears. I can't believe I am doing this.

Eight laps fly by in a hurry. I drop the car into neutral, coast down pit lane and hope I can stop the car where the flagman is directing me to stop. What I know I can't stop is my shaking. My hands, my heart, my whole body is pounding as I climb out of the car. I can't believe it. I have never felt anything like this. And I get to do it again!

On the second set, I don't mind that the track walls fly by in a blur, that I can't tell if the sky is up or down, that I can't remember what turn I am in. All that matters is that I am living a dream.

On the way back to the media center I'm sweating, elated and shaking like a jumping bean as I peel off my racing gear. I can't stay still I am so excited. All of us would-be racers and our families gather together to receive our diplomas and lap speeds. We did it. It's official. And, believe it or not, I beat Clint's time by .53 of a second. I can't wait to do this again!

Cinnamon Logs

This was my favorite cookie as a child and is now my kids' favorite. We call these 'Aunt Hilda's cookies'. Can't eat just one!

- 1 tablespoon vanilla extract
- 3 eggs
- 1 cup vegetable oil
- 1/4 cup milk
- 1 1/2 cups sugar
- 1 tablespoon lemon juice
- 4 tablespoons baking powder
- 1 tablespoon ground cloves
- 2 tablespoons ground cinnamon
- 5 cups flour (more for rolling cookies)

Combine vanilla, eggs, oil, milk, sugar and lemon juice. Set aside. In a separate bowl, combine baking powder, cloves, cinnamon and flour. Fold the dry and wet ingredients together and mix well. Let rest 10 minutes. Roll dough into logs and cut into 1 inch pieces. Bake at 350º until golden, 10-15 minutes.

Icing

- 3 cups powdered sugar
- 8 tablespoons butter, melted
- 1/4 cup milk

Combine ingredients. Dip top of cookies in the icing.

CAT FRIENDS

Looking through the classifieds to find my Siamese cats some twenty years ago, little did I realize the commitment and attachment that comes with having pets. I was young and excited and couldn't wait for the kitties. First came Hershey, a seal point. Then Cameron, a chocolate point. Although my intention was to breed these two full-bred cats, I soon realized that I wasn't a very good candidate for the job. I wanted to keep all six kittens from the very first litter! I settled on keeping one. I named him Rocky, after Rocky Balboa from the movie that was so popular at the time. Today, many years later, Rocky is old and a bit crazy, and still just as vocal as he was as a kitten.

The second litter brought six more kittens. Samba, named for the famous Brazilian dance, became the newest addition to our home. My cat family of four was now complete.

Hershey, Cameron, Rocky and Samba were loved and fed, and clearly had the run of the house. They were so sheltered, I can say with confidence that they never saw a dog. They were as friendly as can be towards our new pet parakeets, oblivious to the fact that the birds were lower on the food chain.

The years went by. Hershey, who we affectionally called "Old Lady" at 22, was still her friendly and demanding self, maneuvering through the house with ease despite total blindness. Rocky and Samba, at 19 and 20 years old, were as frisky as ever. Our house was referred to as the "Assisted Living for Cats."

Then, one by one, the cats became ill. Cameron was the first to go. Next, Samba, who, after many tests and tears, had to be put to sleep. Just two weeks later, Hershey, the matriarch of the family, began to show the signs. Another heart wrenching trip to the vet was almost more than I could take.

Life goes on and now only Rocky remains. He often spends time resting on his big, fluffy heated pillow, wondering where his family has gone. These cats were a part of our lives for more than 22 years, longer than many marriages. Our house seems empty; my supply of cat food and litter is sparse. I miss my cats, but the memories of these wonderful pets fill my heart.

Indulge in your passion! Whether it is cooking or decorating, music or crafts—let your imagination take hold. It's a wonderful thing to get up in the morning and do what you love.

Be grateful. It's important to acknowledge the people and situations in your life. Be thankful for every day; sunny or rainy, each flower in the spring and falling leaves in the autumn. As you look around you will realize all the little things in your life that are truly amazing.

Be honest with yourself and others. Sharing our true feelings gives us the freedom from fear and rejection. Be who you are and surround yourself with the same type of person. You will feel relieved when you don't have to try to be a different person or live up to someone else's expectations.

DRINKS AND PUNCHES

Creative Holiday Punch Ideas and Recipes

- Garnish your punch with slices of star fruit for a festive touch.
- Freeze fresh cranberries in ice cubes for a colorful and cooling idea.
- Freeze red or green grapes to float in your punch.
- Dress up purchased eggnog with french vanilla ice cream and ground nutmeg; add brewed espresso or strong coffee for cappuccino eggnog.

This is a fun chapter. Every party needs a special drink. It is a good idea to offer both an alcohol and a non-alcohol punch at your parties!

Raspberry Sparkle

1 12-ounce can frozen raspberry juice
1 2-liter bottle lemon lime soda
1 cup triple sec
1 magnum spumanti
1 16-ounce package frozen raspberries

Combine all ingredients. Chill and serve in a pretty pitcher.

Champagne Cosmo

1 gallon cranberry juice
2 cups vodka
1 cup triple sec
1 cups orange juice
1/2 cup lime juice
1 magnum spumante

Combine all ingredients. Chill and serve in a pretty pitcher.

Wonderful Warmed Cider

Great for Fall Celebrations.

1 gallon apple cider
2 cups rum
1/2 gallon apple juice
2 cups orange juice
Sprinkle of cinnamon

Combine all ingredients and warm through on low heat. Serve in a pretty pitcher. This should be served warm, not hot!

To make this non-alcoholic, leave out the rum.

Mother's Day Punch

1 quart pineapple juice
1 cup rum
1 quart lemon lime soda
1 cup vodka
1 quart orange juice
1 cup triple sec
2 cups fresh cut strawberries for garnish

Combine all ingredients. Chill and serve in a pretty pitcher.

Springtime Sangria

- 8 cups red wine
- 1 cup triple sec
- 2 cups lemon lime soda
- 1 orange, sliced thin
- 1 lemon, sliced thin
- 1 cup peaches, cut up (you can use thawed frozen peaches)

Combine all ingredients. Chill and serve in a pretty pitcher.

Lemon-Raspberry Margarita

- 1 gallon lemonade
- 2 cups tequila
- 1 cup triple sec
- 1/2 cup lime juice
- 1/2 cup sugar
- 1 cup frozen raspberries

Combine all ingredients. Chill and serve in a pretty pitcher.

Florida Sunshine

- 2 cups vodka
- 4 cups orange juice
- 1 cup triple sec
- 1 2-liter bottle lemon lime soda

Combine all ingredients. Chill and serve in a pretty pitcher.

Raspberry Tea Punch

- 1 12-ounce can frozen raspberry cocktail, defrosted
- 1 gallon sweetened iced tea
- 1 2-liter bottle lemon lime soda

Combine all ingredients. Chill and serve in a pretty pitcher.

THE MAN IN THE PEACH THONG

We noticed him first at the airport. We'd landed at Montego Bay after a holding pattern due to the low visibility and soaking rains over Jamaica. The airport was a mess: puddles of water at every turn, buckets and yellow caution signs everywhere, rain-soaked tourists and natives alike standing in lines for immigration that seemed to stand still.

We kept our calm. What could we do? Nothing really, except stand in line and wait our turn. Finally through immigration and customs, we faced yet another delay. Our connecting flight on a little "puddle jumper" plane destined for Negril was grounded. The puddles were too big today. The roads to Negril were eventually closed due to the heavy rain. We were sent a short 10 minutes away to Breezes in Montego Bay until the transportation authorities could figure out what to do with us. The resort was packed full of wet, irritable people and suitcases, all destined for elsewhere.

We spotted him again. Familiar faces, he and his wife. We were trying to place him. We knew we'd seen him on a nude beach—that's not something easily forgotten. But where? Was it the long, quiet Orient Beach on St. Martin where we'd stayed many times before or here in Jamaica?

Not a social couple when we vacation, we prefer just to observe and people watch. It's fun to do. We'd seen this elderly, white-haired gentleman before; his wife walks with a bit of a limp. He always seemed to us to be quoting Shakespeare in his rich British accent, a professor for sure.

He seemed to recognize us as well. We exchanged smiles. I knew that eventually we would remember where we had seen him before. The rain subsided. The three-hour wait for our hotel was coming to an end. Wet and tired, we were herded onto a tiny bus bound for Negril. On the bus I had a chance to speak to our friend. He had recognized us from here, in Jamaica, on one of his frequent trips. We could place him now, walking down the beach, head held high, big glasses perched on his nose, acknowledging fellow sun worshippers.

A surprise awaited us the next morning when we arrived at the beach bar for coffee. He was there—in very appropriate attire for the beaches of Negril. Our professor—in a peach thong!

COWBOY LOVE

Nearing sunset, the Caribbean is quiet. The water laps gently on the beach. The hot tub is still at last. Most people have left the beach. Dinner is a few hours away. We sit on our patio, overlooking the beach, a drink in hand, just enjoying this time of day—a smoky, dusky, vanishing sunlight.

A sound gently takes shape. It's coming from above. Pouring out of the sky, notes gently catch the breeze. A strong male country voice, singing...we can barely make out the words...lamenting, pouring out his heart. He sings of "Cowboy Love." Island charm with a western touch. After a while the music stops, quietness descends upon us, the air is suddenly empty. We sit there disappointed, wanting more.

Gradually, there is more activity as people start to go to dinner. We sit sipping the last of our drinks. From around the corner, in the early shadow of night, comes a lone, tall, strong figure. Pointy snakeskin boots, white shirt tucked into tight jeans and the biggest cowboy hat you have every seen. He strolls towards the beach, his back to us. As when cowboys roamed the West, romance and adventure surround him as he strolls toward the sunset. It's cowboy love, live in person, in the Caribbean. (And I only had ONE drink!)

Nut Cracker Sweet

Perfect punch for that holiday party.

- 1 gallon apple juice
- 4 cups cranberry juice
- 1/4 cup honey
- Dash cinnamon
- 2 cinnamon sticks

Combine all ingredients and warm on low heat. Serve this warm, not hot, in a pretty pitcher.

White Christmas

- 1 cup Irish cream liqueur
- 1 cup coffee liqueur
- 1 cup vodka
- 1 quart softened vanilla ice cream
- Ice cubes

Combine all ingredients in blender. Drink it slowly or you'll be lying in the snow!

"What a difference a day makes, 24 little hours," Ella Fitzgerald sang that song so well! Oh, how that statement is so true. Anger, stress, sadness, anxiety, helplessness, fear…all those feelings can be reduced by taking a step back and letting a day go by. It will give you another perspective. Sleep on it, like they say! Take a day, 24 little hours, and see what a difference it can make. Our lives are filled with days and minutes. It can all make a difference. So take a day…for you!

Look in the mirror every morning and tell yourself that you are beautiful, strong, creative, energetic and confident. Get rid of all those negative thoughts that keep popping into our heads! They bring us down and lower our self-esteem. Make a list of all those attributes you admire and repeat them to yourself daily! It will change your life.

Have a sanctuary or quiet place in your home that you can go to when you need to relax or work out a problem. A favorite chair, a sunny windowsill or a back door step. A place that feels comfortable to you and brings you peace and security.

LET'S HAVE A PARTY

My favorite time of year is autumn. The colors, flavors and seasonal foods are exceptional. Hearty meals, soups and stews, mashed potatoes with carmelized garlic, pot roast, short ribs of beef—these are comfort foods, bringing back memories of meals gone by. Food comforts us when all else fails, filling our tummies and souls with the warmth and color that is autumn. It soothes us in times of need, fills a place in our hearts, and allows us to create and share memories. Comfort foods are often easy to prepare—one big pot simmering on the stove, filling the house with a wonderful aroma—the fragrance of love and caring. Make a big pot of soup and share it with everyone. It will be sure to make you feel great!

Barbecue Pork Quesadillas

- 1 lb. shredded pork
- 1 cup barbecue sauce
- 1/4 cup chopped cilantro
- 5 scallions, chopped
- 1 cup shredded cheddar cheese
- 8 flour tortillas

Rinse pork and pat dry. Lay on cookie sheet sprayed with cooking spray and roast uncovered at 350º for 20-25 minutes. Cool, slice and shred. Combine shredded pork with remaining 4 ingredients. Fill 1/2 tortilla shell and fold over. Cook on both sides in nonstick sauté pan sprayed with cooking spray. Cook remaining tortillas, let cool, then cut into wedges. Reheat covered at 350º for 10-15 minutes.

Pear and Walnut Salad

- 1 15-ounce can pears, cut into pieces (reserve 1/4 cup juice for vinaigrette)
- 5-6 cups mixed greens

Vinaigrette

- 1 shallot, chopped
- 1 tablespoon Dijon mustard
- 2 tablespoons red wine vinegar
- Kosher salt and fresh cracked pepper to taste
- 1/4 cup pear juice (reserved from canned pears)
- 1 tablespoon honey
- 1 cup olive oil

Sugared Nuts

- 1 cup walnuts
- 2 tablespoons butter
- 2 tablespoons brown sugar

Place mixed greens in salad bowl. Combine all vinaigrette ingredients in food processor, adding oil last. Process until mixed, 2-3 minutes. Melt butter in sauté pan. Add walnuts and brown sugar. Remove from heat and stir well. Top mixed greens with vinaigrette, sugared walnuts and pears.

Asparagus with Buttered Pine Nuts

2 lbs. asparagus
1 cup pine nuts
4 tablespoons butter, melted
Kosher salt and fresh cracked pepper to taste
1 teaspoon granulated garlic

Clean and cut off ends of asparagus. Boil or steam, cooking until tender, 5-7 minutes. Sauté pine nuts in melted butter with salt, pepper and garlic, until golden. Pour over cooked asparagus. Heat uncovered at 350º for 10-15 minutes.

Mushroom and Potato Gratin

2 lbs. red bliss potatoes
3 cloves garlic, minced
2-3 tablespoons butter
2 tablespoons olive oil
4 cups sliced mushrooms
Kosher salt and fresh cracked pepper to taste
1/4 cup flour
1/4 cup chicken broth
1/2 cup heavy cream
2 cups grated cheddar cheese

Cook potatoes in unsalted water until tender, 5-10 minutes. Drain and rinse well. Cut into 1/4 inch slices. Sauté garlic and mushrooms in butter and oil. Season with salt and pepper and cook until soft. Add flour. Combine until mixed. Add cream and chicken broth. Layer potatoes, mushrooms and cheese. Repeat. Bake at 350º for 25-30 minutes. Uncover the last 10 minutes.

Savoy Cabbage with Ham

2 heads savoy cabbage (curly cabbage) rinsed and cut into chunks
8 cloves garlic (keep whole)
1/2 cup olive oil
Kosher salt and fresh cracked pepper to taste
1 ham butt, cut into chunks (about 2 lbs.)
1 tablespoon brown sugar
1 teaspoon celery seeds

Sauté garlic for 5 minutes in oil. Add cabbage and season with salt and pepper. Cook covered over high heat until reduced, 10-15 minutes. Add ham, celery seeds and sugar. Cover and heat at 350º for 30-40 additional minutes.

Bubbly Hot Blue Cheese Dip

Serve with celery sticks, bread slices, crudité—or just eat it with a spoon!

1 cup mayonnaise
1 cup blue cheese
1/2 cup shredded cheddar cheese
Dash of hot sauce
1/2 cup chopped onion

Combine all ingredients together and pour into ovenproof dish. Bake uncovered at 350º for 20-30 minutes until bubbly.

Did you make too much food? Share it with a neighbor who lives alone, the postman or a friend. Everyone loves a meal someone else made! Make a big pot of soup and you'll have lots of friends!

Chicken Cassoulet

10 skinless, boneless chicken thighs
3-4 tablespoons olive oil
2 tablespoons butter
2 8-ounce packages mushrooms
1 large onion, chopped
2 teaspoons chopped garlic
1 teaspoon dried rosemary
Kosher salt and fresh cracked pepper to taste
1/2 cup vermouth
1 10-ounce can mushroom soup
1 40-ounce can white beans, rinsed and drained
1 cup fresh breadcrumbs
3 tablespoons butter, melted
1/2 cup grated Parmesan cheese

Sauté chicken in butter and oil until brown, only about 5 minutes on each side. Season with salt and pepper. Remove and set aside. In same sauté pan, add mushrooms, onion, garlic and rosemary. Add vermouth and cream of mushroom soup. Combine until smooth. Toss in beans, mix together, and pour over chicken in ovenproof dish. Combine breadcrumbs, Parmesan cheese and melted butter. Sprinkle on top of chicken. Cover and bake at 350º for 40 minutes. Uncover and bake an additional 30 minutes.

To make fresh breadcrumbs, use rolls, soft bread or sandwich bread and chop coarsely in a food processor. Store in freezer. Use in recipes such as stuffed mushrooms, crabcakes and meatballs.

Pumpkin Bread Pudding

2 loaves cinnamon bread, cut diagonally
1 quart light cream
6 eggs
1 15-ounce can pumpkin
1 stick butter, cut up
1 1/2 cups brown sugar

Whisk together light cream, eggs and canned pumpkin. Layer 1/2 of bread, sugar, butter and cream mix. Repeat. Cover and bake at 350º for 45-55 minutes.

Vanilla Sauce

Add brandy for extra flavor.

1 5.1-ounce box instant vanilla pudding
1 1/4 cup milk
2 cups heavy cream

Whisk sauce ingredients together until smooth. Serve in a pretty bowl to drizzle over warm bread pudding.

With the popularity of the cooking channel, kids in the kitchen is inevitable. Suddenly everyone wants to cook—whether participating by setting the table, stirring ingredients in a bowl or baking cookies. Creativity abounds in a warm friendly kitchen. As a child I remember rolling out the pasta dough, frying the meatballs and tasting the sauce. Learning early on that there was much to do in the kitchen, I was eager to be a part of it. I accompanied my mother to the butchers and the chicken man, and went out to the local huckster to pick the best produce. Now with my grandchildren, I am eager to share my love of food. My motto is, 'Teach a child to cook and you will teach a child to eat.' They will be more eager to try something that they have a part in creating. Keep it simple but make it fun. Cook with your little ones. They will delight you with their enthusiasm and curiosity.

Caesar Salad

Romaine lettuce, torn into bite-sized pieces
1/2 cup grated Parmesan cheese
2 cloves garlic, minced
1 tablespoon Dijon mustard
1 cup olive oil
Kosher salt and fresh cracked pepper to taste

Combine dressing ingredients in a container and shake well. Mix thoroughly with romaine lettuce and croutons.

Croutons

2 cups bread cubes
1/2 cup olive oil
1/2 cup grated Parmesan cheese
Kosher salt and fresh cracked pepper to taste

Toss crouton ingredients together. Bake at 350º for 10-15 minutes until golden.

Pastry Wrapped Franks with Honey Mustard

1 lb. package hot dogs
1 pack refrigerated crescent rolls

Roll hot dogs with crescent rolls. Cut into 4 pieces. Put on a cookie sheet and bake uncovered at 350º for 10-15 minutes.

Honey Mustard

1 cup mustard
2 tablespoons honey

Mix together to make a honey mustard sauce for dipping.

Pizza

Kids love to make pizza. They can personalize it with their favorite toppings.

- Pre-baked pizza piecrust
- 1 tablespoon olive oil
- 1 cup marinara sauce
- Grated cheese
- Assorted toppings (broccoli, olives, pepperoni)

Rub oil on crust. Top with marinara, cheese and your favorite toppings. Bake at 350º uncovered for 20 minutes.

When having kids make pizza, I like to have an assortment of cheeses—mozzarella, Parmesan and even cheddar.

Smashed Potatoes with Cheddar and Bacon

- 3 lbs. potatoes, cut into 1/4" slices
- 1 cup half and half
- 1 stick butter
- Kosher salt and fresh cracked pepper to taste
- 1 cup grated cheddar cheese
- 4-6 slices bacon, cooked and crumbled

Cook potatoes in salted water until tender. Drain. While potatoes are still hot, add half & half and butter. Season with salt and pepper. Add grated cheese and bacon. Mix well.

Chicken Strips

Use one hand for wet ingredients and one hand for dry—no mess!

- 1 lb. boneless chicken breast, cut into strips
- 1 egg
- 1/4 cup milk
- 2 cups bread crumbs

Mix egg and milk. Dip chicken in milk and egg mixture. Roll in breadcrumbs. Put on baking sheet sprayed with cooking spray. Bake at 350º for 15-20 minutes or until golden.

Two Dipping Sauces for Chicken

Barbecue Sauce

- 1 cup ketchup
- 2 tablespoons vinegar
- 2 teaspoons Worcestershire sauce
- 1 tablespoon hot sauce
- 1/2 cup water
- 1/2 cup brown sugar
- 1 teaspoon chili powder

Combine all ingredients in saucepan and heat until well blended.

Honey Dijon Raspberry Mustard

- 1/2 cup honey
- 1 cup Dijon mustard
- 1 cup mayonnaise
- 1 tablespoon raspberry preserves

Combine all ingredients until well blended.

Hate peas? Can't stand asparagus? Don't like hamburgers? We all have different tastes. Sometimes a particular displeasure for food can stem from a childhood experience or just plain bad cooking! Give those foods another try. Our tastes change over the years. Broaden your horizon and be adventurous with your palate. Try it! You might like it!

Pasta with Ricotta Sauce

It is best to use whole milk ricotta for a wonderful rich flavor.

1 lb. pasta, cooked
1 tablespoon olive oil
1 teaspoon kosher salt
2 cups ricotta cheese
1/2 cup heavy cream
2 cups marinara sauce
1/4 cup grated Parmesan cheese

Cook pasta. Mix with olive oil and kosher salt. Mix hot pasta with ricotta cheese and cream. Add marinara sauce and Parmesan cheese. Put in baking dish and cover. Bake covered at 350º for 20-25 minutes.

Brownies with Ice Cream and Fudge Sauce

Serve these yummy brownies with vanilla ice cream, whipped cream and sprinkles.

Bake a box of brownie mix according to package directions. Let cool. Cut into circles with cookie cutter.

Fudge Sauce

1 cup chocolate chips
1 cup heavy cream

Combine chocolate chips and cream in saucepan until melted. Use a whisk to blend easily.

My kids are always saying that there is nothing to eat at my house. Now I know this sounds funny, but when they open my refrigerator or freezer they tell me there are only ingredients! The freezer is a great place to store ingredients—grated cheese, nuts, coffee beans, breadcrumbs. All will last longer and have more flavor if stored in the freezer. With fresh, delicious ingredients you can always make something great to eat!

Asian Influence

Growing up Italian, I know the importance of food and flavor. As a child, my parents would take us downtown to Chinatown to enjoy and appreciate another, very different, culture. Believe it or not, we would go as a family—aunts, uncles and cousins, all seated at a long table and trying all different kinds of Asian food. It was quite an experience, although my father was always looking for bread! I came to appreciate and love Asian cooking. To this day we enjoy it at least once a week. In my lifetime the world has gotten smaller. There are many wonderful flavors and adventures to try. So take a trip, a culinary trip, and try something different. Be adventurous!

Vegetable Stir Fry with Teriyaki Glaze

5 cups cut up assorted vegetables (snow peas, broccoli, carrots, red peppers, asparagus, zucchini)

Teriyaki Glaze

1 cup soy sauce
1/4 cup mirin
1/2 cup water
1/4 cup brown sugar
2 teaspoons chopped garlic
2 teaspoons chopped ginger
Kosher salt and fresh cracked pepper to taste
1 tablespoon cornstarch
2 tablespoons water

To make glaze, combine all ingredients except cornstarch and water, in saucepan. Bring to a boil. Lower heat. Combine cornstarch and water to make a paste. Whisk cornstarch mix into glaze until thick. In wok or large sauté pan, combine teriyaki glaze with vegetables over high heat. Serve with rice.

Mirin is a sweet liquid cooking seasoning that can be used in place of sugar and honey. It is found in the Asian section of your local supermarket.

Five Spice Salmon with Coconut Glaze

This coconut glaze can be used for any type of fish.

1 side of salmon, skin removed (approx. 3-3 1/2 lbs.)
1/2 cup brown sugar
1/2 cup soy sauce
3 tablespoons chopped scallions
2 tablespoons chopped ginger
1/2 teaspoon sesame oil
Pinch of five-spice powder
1/2 cup canned coconut milk

Combine all glaze ingredients and pour over salmon. Roast uncovered at 350º for 25-30 minutes.

Five-spice powder is a mixture of cinnamon, star anise, fennel, cloves and ginger. It has a slightly sweet smelling pungent flavor.

Chicken Skewers With Trio of Dipping Sauces

1 lb. boneless chicken breast, cleaned and cut into strips

6-inch bamboo skewers

Thread chicken strips on skewers. Layer on cookie sheet and bake uncovered at 350º for 15-20 minutes. Remove and set aside. When ready to serve, display cooked chicken skewers with sauces.

Hot Mustard Dip

4 tablespoons hot mustard powder

2 tablespoon water

2 tablespoons soy sauce

4 tablespoons mayonnaise

Combine all ingredients and mix well.

Honey Wasabi Sauce

2 tablespoons wasabi paste (mix together 1 tablespoon wasabi powder and 2 tablespoons water to form paste)

1/4 cup honey

1 cup mayonnaise

3 tablespoons sour cream

Kosher salt and fresh cracked pepper to taste

Combine all ingredients and mix well.

Sweet and Sour Cucumber Sauce

1/2 cup white vinegar

1/4 cup water

1/4 cup sugar

Kosher salt to taste

3 cucumbers, peeled and seeded

1 teaspoon chopped ginger

Combine all ingredients in food processor and process until chunky.

Crab Stir Fry

1 lb. jumbo lump crabmeat

1 cup sliced vegetables (any combination of onions, celery, peppers and mushrooms)

2 tablespoons olive oil

1 tablespoon chopped garlic

1 teaspoon chopped ginger

3 tablespoons soy sauce

1/2 cup chopped tomatoes

1 teaspoon tomato sauce

1/2 cup chicken broth

Sauté garlic, ginger and vegetables in hot oil. Add remaining ingredients and cook 10-15 minutes. Can be served over rice.

Oriental Pasta Salad

1 lb. long pasta, cooked and drained

2 cups assorted vegetables (carrots, yellow squash, broccoli, red pepper, asparagus)

1 cup olive oil (reserve 2 tablespoons to sauté vegetables)

1/2 cup teriyaki or soy sauce

1/2 cup brown sugar

2 tablespoons minced ginger

2 cloves garlic, chopped

Dash hot sauce

Kosher salt and fresh cracked pepper to taste

Sauté vegetables lightly in oil. Combine pasta and vegetables. Set aside. Whisk together remaining ingredients to make dressing. Toss with pasta and vegetables. Serve cold.

I always use thin spaghetti when making this pasta salad.

Hosting an outdoor party can be more work then popping a casserole in the oven, so it's important to be prepared. Sauces and marinades can be prepared in advance. I also like to precook some of the meat that will be grilled, ensuring a shorter cooking time on the grill as well as consistent doneness. Don't be afraid to make salads and dressings ahead, keeping them separate until the morning of your party and then tossing them together and displaying them in a pretty bowl. Don't serve out of plastic containers. Remember that food always tastes better if it looks good. Presentation is half of it—you eat with your eyes first! Although the cooking is done outdoors, present and display your food indoors, allowing more control over outdoor temperature and bugs!

Tequila Salsa Fresca

If making ahead of time, cut up dry ingredients and keep them separate from the liquid ingredients. Combine them just before serving.

6 plum tomatoes, diced
1 red onion, diced
2-3 hot peppers, chopped
1 clove garlic, minced
1/4 cup chopped cilantro or Italian flat leaf parsley
3 tablespoons lime juice
1 teaspoon honey
2 tablespoons tequila
1 tablespoon olive oil
Kosher salt and fresh cracked pepper to taste

Combine ingredients for salsa. Serve with tortilla chips.

Tossed Salad with Orange Mustard Dressing

This makes a wonderful dressing for grilled vegetables.

Fresh Greens
Red Onions
Sliced Apples
Diced Celery

Dressing

1/2 cup orange juice
2 tablespoons lime juice
2 tablespoons vinegar
2 tablespoons Dijon mustard
2 tablespoons honey
1 cup olive oil
Kosher salt and fresh cracked pepper

Combine dressing ingredients in container and shake well. Pour over salad.

To save time, put your lettuce in your pretty salad bowl and cover it with a damp paper towel. It will stay crisp for a few hours without refrigeration.

Oriental Green Bean Salad

2 lbs. green beans, cooked

Dressing

1/2 cup soy sauce
1/4 cup rice vinegar
1 tablespoon minced garlic
1/4 cup sesame seeds
1 tablespoon cup sesame oil
1 tablespoon minced fresh ginger
4 scallions, chopped
2 tablespoons olive oil

Whisk dressing ingredients together in bowl. Toss with green beans and serve.

Grilled Corn with Lime Butter and Seasoned Salt

1 cup butter, softened
1/4 cup lime juice
Kosher salt and fresh cracked pepper to taste
12 ears corn, husked

Cook corn in boiling water for 5 minutes, and then grill, turning until golden, about 5 minutes. Blend together softened butter, lime juice, salt and pepper. Chill. Serve lime butter and seasoned salt with cooked corn.

Grilled Asparagus with Vinaigrette

When grilling, asparagus with a thicker stalk is easiest to use.

3 lbs. asparagus, blanched and grilled

Vinaigrette

1 cup olive oil
2-3 tablespoons lemon juice
1 tablespoon minced garlic
1 pint grape tomatoes, rinsed
2 tablespoons chopped Italian flat leaf parsley
Kosher salt and fresh cracked pepper to taste

Toss together ingredients for vinaigrette. Drizzle over grilled asparagus.

To blanch asparagus, bring water to a boil in a large sauté pan. Add asparagus and when water resumes boiling, drain and remove asparagus. This takes about 5 minutes. Asparagus is easier to grill once blanched.

Seasoned Salt

Can be used with grilled vegetables, meats and seafood. It adds a delicious flavor.

1 cup kosher salt
1/4 cup black pepper
1 tablespoon white pepper
1 tablespoon cayenne pepper
1 tablespoon sugar

Combine all ingredients. This can be stored in your spice cabinet for up to 6 months.

Some spices have been in our cabinets since our first wedding anniversary! Dried spices lose their flavors quickly. Go through your cabinets and throw out anything over a year old. You probably can't figure out what it is anyway! Refresh your spices and your food will thank you.

Cowboy Beans

1 40-ounce can dark red beans
1 40-ounce can light red beans
1 40-ounce can white beans
1/4 cup olive oil
2 large onions, diced
2 cloves garlic, minced
1/4 cup vinegar
1 teaspoon chili powder
Dash hot sauce
2 cups ketchup
1 cup beer
Kosher salt and fresh cracked pepper to taste

Drain and rinse beans. Set aside. Sauté onion and garlic in hot oil, 5-7 minutes. Combine remaining ingredients in saucepan and heat 20-30 minutes, stirring occasionally, or place all ingredients in a casserole dish, cover and bake at 350º for 30 minutes.

Blue Cheese Burgers

2 lbs. ground beef
1 cup crumbled blue cheese
1 teaspoon thyme
2 cloves garlic, minced
Kosher salt and fresh cracked pepper to taste

Mix all ingredients. Form patties and chill. Grill until desired doneness is reached.

Beef Ribs with Bourbon Shallot Sauce

5 lbs. beef ribs

Dry Rub

Combine 1 teaspoon each of pepper, salt, paprika, garlic powder, cayenne pepper, allspice and celery seeds.

Extra dry rub can be stored up to 3 months in spice cabinet.

Bourbon Shallot Sauce

1 cup bourbon
2-3 shallots, minced
1 red onion, minced
4 cloves garlic
1 cup ketchup
1/2 cup cider vinegar
1/2 cup brown sugar
Kosher salt and fresh cracked pepper to taste

Heat together sauce ingredients over low heat for 5-10 minutes. Dust ribs with 1-2 tablespoons dry rub. Pour sauce over dry rubbed beef ribs. Roast covered at 350º for 2 1/2 hours.

Royal Rum Punch

1/2 gallon orange juice
1 cup rum
Sliced lemons and oranges
1/2 gallon fruit punch
1/2 cup triple sec
4 cups pineapple juice

Combine all ingredients and serve in a pitcher.

Cajun Rum Barbecue Turkey

4-5 lbs. turkey breast

Ragin' Cajun Turkey Rub

Combine 1 tablespoon each kosher salt, black pepper, thyme, garlic powder, paprika, cayenne pepper and onion powder

Rub 2-3 tablespoons rub mix onto turkey breast. Roast at 350º for 25-35 minutes and then grill for an additional 5 minutes on each side.

Extra turkey rub can be stored up to 3 months in spice cabinet.

Cajun Rum Barbecue Sauce

2 cups ketchup
1/3 cup rum
1/4 cup vinegar
1/4 cup honey
2 cloves garlic, minced
1 tablespoon hot pepper sauce
2 tablespoons soy sauce
1/4 cup pineapple juice
Kosher salt and fresh cracked pepper to taste

Combine ingredients in saucepan and heat for 10-15 minutes. Serve with Cajun turkey.

Grilled Lamb Skewers with Coconut-Ginger Sauce

2-3 lbs. lamb, cut into chunks
1 teaspoon curry powder
1 teaspoon kosher salt
1 teaspoon pepper
1 teaspoon cayenne pepper
2-3 tablespoons olive oil

Combine ingredients to make marinade. Toss with lamb chunks. While the lamb is marinating, soak the bamboo skewers in water for 1/2 hour. Thread lamb on skewers. Bake at 350º for 15-20 minutes, then transfer lamb skewers to grill. Grill 5 minutes on each side.

Coconut-Ginger Sauce

1 tablespoon olive oil
1 teaspoon sesame oil
2 tablespoons minced ginger
1 tablespoon minced garlic
1 teaspoon hot sauce or chili paste
1 12-ounce can coconut milk
2 tablespoons lime juice
2 tablespoons chopped cilantro

Sauté ginger, garlic and hot sauce in mixed oils. Add remaining ingredients and heat through. Pour over grilled lamb kabobs or serve as a dipping sauce.

Coconut milk can be found in the specialty aisle of your local supermarket.

London Broil with Honey Balsamic-Dijon Glaze

2-3 lbs. London broil

Dry Rub

Combine 1 tablespoon each of pepper, salt, paprika, garlic powder, cayenne pepper, allspice and celery seeds.

Rub London broil with 2-3 tablespoons dry rub. Cook at 350º for 15-20 minutes. Transfer to grill and cook until desired doneness is reached.

Extra dry rub can be stored for up to 3 months in spice cabinet.

Honey Balsamic-Dijon Glaze

1 cup cider vinegar
1/2 cup honey
1/2 cup Dijon mustard
1/2 cup balsamic vinegar
1/4 cup corn syrup
2 tablespoons lemon juice
2 tablespoons tomato paste
1 teaspoon garlic powder
Dash hot sauce
Kosher salt and fresh cracked pepper to taste

Combine glaze ingredients in pan and sauté for 15-20 minutes. Serve with grilled London broil.

London broil is a cut of meat that requires a long, slow cooking time in the oven or a short cooking time on a grill. Check meat with a cooking thermometer until desired internal temperature is reached.

Cucumber Relish

1 clove garlic, whole
1/3 cup white vinegar
1/3 cup sugar
Kosher salt to taste
4 cucumbers, peeled, seeded and diced
Sprinkle of red pepper flakes
1/2 cup diced red onion
Sprinkle of chopped Italian flat leaf parsley

Mix garlic, vinegar and sugar together in saucepan. Heat on low until sugar is dissolved. Let cool. Discard garlic. Combine remaining ingredients with white vinegar mixture.

Onion Jam

This recipe can be prepared one week in advance.

3 large onions, sliced thin
2 tablespoons butter, melted
1 cup diced red onion
1 cup chopped scallions
1/4 cup balsamic vinegar
1/4 cup brown sugar

Sauté ingredients in melted butter, covered for the first 15 minutes. Remove cover and continue cooking on low until golden, about 20 minutes. Serve at room temperature as a topping for hamburger or grilled steak.

The holidays are typically stressful. Family and friends gather to celebrate, but behind the scenes in the kitchen can be a very busy place. It's important to have a plan, make a list and give yourself plenty of time. Do as much as you can ahead of time. Get out your dishes and serving pieces. Look over your menu and shop for ingredients in advance. Prepare your food in ovenproof pottery dishes so you won't have to transfer from pan to dish, doubling the clean up time. Pre-cook your casserole for half the cooking time the day before, allowing your food to come to room temperature before reheating. Remember never to tell anyone your mistakes and, finally, accept all offers of help. Be good to yourself. Enjoy the companionship of this celebration and keep a sense of humor. It always helps to laugh!

Creamy Cheddar Broccoli

2 heads broccoli, cut up and cooked
2 tablespoons butter
2 tablespoons flour
2 cups warmed milk
2 cups shredded cheddar cheese
1/2 cup grated Parmesan cheese
Kosher salt and fresh cracked pepper to taste

Heat butter in saucepan. Add flour and mix until it forms a paste, 5-10 minutes. Warm milk in microwave or on the stove over low heat. Whisk in warmed milk until thick. Add cheddar and Parmesan cheese and season with salt and pepper. Stir until melted. Top broccoli with cheese mixture and bake covered at 350º for 20-25 minutes.

When you are trying to keep a casserole hot after it is removed from the oven, dishtowels are your best friends. Layer them on top of foil-wrapped, oven-hot casserole dishes and they will act as a layer of clothing to keep your food piping hot.

Green Beans with Leeks and Garlic

1 tablespoon butter
4 tablespoons olive oil
2 tablespoons leeks, sliced
6 cloves garlic, whole
1 teaspoon honey
Kosher salt and fresh cracked pepper to taste
2 lbs. green beans, cooked in unsalted water 5-7 minutes or until done

Sauté leeks and garlic in butter and oil until soft and golden. Season with salt and pepper. Add honey. Toss with green beans.

When cooking green beans, never cover the pot. It will turn your beans gray.

Cassis Glazed Carrots with Tarragon

4 cups baby carrots, cooked until tender
3 tablespoons butter
1 teaspoon dried tarragon
1 tablespoon brown sugar
1-2 tablespoons cassis (berry) liqueur
Kosher salt and fresh cracked pepper to taste

Sauté tarragon and brown sugar in butter. Add cassis. Season with salt and pepper. Toss with carrots.

Glazed Sweet Potatoes, Apples and Brandy with Cardamom

Macintosh apples work best with this recipe. Regular brandy or apple juice can be substituted for apple brandy.

2 40-ounce cans sweet potatoes, drained and rinsed
1 stick butter, melted
2 tablespoons light corn syrup
1/4 cup brown sugar
1 teaspoon cardamom
4 apples, sliced
2 tablespoons apple brandy
Kosher salt and fresh cracked pepper to taste

Add corn syrup and brown sugar to melted butter. Add apples and sauté. Add brandy. Season with salt, pepper and cardamon. Pour apple mixture over sweet potatoes. Bake covered at 350º for 20-30 minutes.

When cooking with apples, I leave the skin on. Remove the grocery sticker and wash them well before slicing.

Asparagus with Mushrooms and Parmesan Cheese

2 lbs. asparagus, trimmed
2 tablespoons olive oil
1 tablespoon butter
1/4 cup Madeira wine
2 cloves garlic, chopped
1 lb. mushrooms
1/4 cup sun-dried tomatoes
2 tablespoons chopped Italian flat leaf parsley
Kosher salt and fresh cracked pepper to taste
1/4 cup grated Parmesan cheese

Boil or steam asparagus until tender, 5-7 minutes. Sauté garlic, mushrooms, sun-dried tomatoes and parsley in butter and oil for 10-15 minutes. Add Madeira wine. Season with salt and pepper. Pour over cooked asparagus and sprinkle with Parmesan cheese. If making ahead, reheat covered at 350º for 15-20 minutes.

Double Cranberry and Orange Sauce

This recipe can be prepared one week ahead and stored in the refrigerator.

1/4 cup triple sec
1/4 cup orange juice
2 bags whole fresh cranberries, rinsed
1 cup sweetened dried cranberries
2 cups sugar
1 can mandarin orange slices with syrup

Simmer all ingredients together in saucepan until thick, about 20-25 minutes.

"Susan's" Savory Family Stuffing

I always prepare my stuffing in a pottery dish instead of stuffing my turkey.

1 lb. Italian sausage, removed from casing, browned and crumbled
12 cups stuffing mix (1/2 corn bread mix and 1/2 seasoned bread mix)
1 1/2 cups chicken broth
2 large eggs
1 stick butter, melted
1 1/2 cups chopped onion
1 1/2 cups chopped celery
1 lb. white mushrooms, chopped
1/4 lb. proscuitto, finely chopped
1 teaspoon minced fresh thyme
1 teaspoon poultry seasoning
1/3 cup chopped Italian flat leaf parsley
Kosher salt and fresh cracked pepper to taste

Mix together chicken broth and eggs. Set aside. Sauté onion, celery, mushrooms and proscuitto in melted butter until soft and glazed. Add thyme, poultry seasoning, parsley, salt and pepper. Add cooked sausage. Toss together with chicken broth mixture and stuffing mixture. Heat covered at 350º for 20-25 minutes.

Proscuitto is an Italian cooked ham. Cooked bacon makes a good substitute.

Turkey with Maple Glaze

4-5 lbs. boneless breast of turkey
1 stick butter, melted
1/2 cup maple syrup
1/4 cup Dijon mustard
1/4 cup chicken broth
Kosher salt and fresh cracked pepper to taste

Cook turkey uncovered at 350º until internal temperature reaches 160º. Combine remaining ingredients for glaze. Pour glaze over turkey during the last hour of cooking.

Always preheat your oven to the specified temperature prior to baking and roasting.

When was the last time you checked that your oven temperature was correct? Buy an oven thermometer and use it so you can be sure that when you set your dial at 350º it's not cooking your food at 425º!

A fun way to entertain! This chapter is about different flavors. With some basic main dishes you can liven up your party by giving your guests a myriad of tastes. I love to eat this way. Offering different possibilities for a variety of tastes will surprise the palate and delight your guests. You can have an adventure in eating. Be sure to label all your sauces and encourage everyone to try all, even though they think they might not like it. They will be surprised at the combinations and enjoy the surprise of flavors.

Marvelous Mashed Potatoes with Toppings

3 lbs. red bliss or Yukon gold potatoes, cut into slices
1 cup heavy cream
6 tablespoons butter
Kosher salt and fresh cracked pepper to taste

Cook potatoes in salted water until soft, 15-20 minutes. Drain and smash together with remaining ingredients. Serve potatoes with these two sauces as toppings.

Grain Mustard and Horseradish Sauce

1 cup mayonnaise
2 tablespoons grain mustard
1 tablespoon horseradish

Combine ingredients and serve chilled.

Spicy Béarnaise

1/2 cup milk
1 envelope (about .9 ounces) powdered béarnaise
1 stick butter, melted
1 tablespoon chili paste or hot sauce
1/2 cup mayonnaise

In melted butter, whisk in envelope of powdered béarnaise sauce. Add milk and simmer until thick. Whisk in chili paste and mayonnaise. Serve chilled.

Roasted Pork Tenderloin with Trio of Sauces

2 packages pork tenderloins (4 pieces)
Kosher salt and fresh cracked pepper to taste

Rinse pork and pat dry. Roast uncovered at 350º for 30-35 minutes. Let cool and slice.

Orange Dijon Glaze

3 tablespoons butter
2 cloves garlic, minced
3 tablespoons orange marmalade
3 tablespoons Dijon mustard
3 tablespoons mayonnaise

Sauté garlic in butter until fragrant. Whisk in remaining ingredients.

Spicy Sweet Carmelized Onions

3 cups thinly sliced onion
4 tablespoons butter, melted
1 tablespoon brown sugar
1 tablespoon hot sauce
Kosher salt and fresh cracked pepper to taste

Sauté onions in butter until golden, 10-15 minutes. Season with salt and pepper. Add sugar and hot sauce.

Roasted Salmon with a Trio of Sauces

Serve your salmon with these 3 side sauces for a fun dinner party.

1 side of salmon, skin removed (approx. 3-3 1/2 pounds)
Kosher salt and fresh cracked pepper to taste

In ovenproof pottery dish, roast salmon uncovered at 350º for 20-30 minutes.

Lemon Pepper Aioli

4 cloves garlic, minced
1 tablespoon lemon juice
2 cups mayonnaise
Kosher salt and fresh cracked pepper to taste

Whisk together ingredients. Serve chilled.

Pepper Relish

2 tablespoons olive oil
2 red peppers, sliced thin
1 yellow or green pepper, sliced thin
1 red onion, sliced thin
1-2 tablespoons red wine vinegar
1 tablespoon brown sugar
Kosher salt and fresh cracked pepper to taste

Combine all ingredients in saucepan and cook until peppers and onions are soft, about 20 minutes. Serve at room temperature.

Olive Tapenade

1 cup stuffed green olives
1 cup pitted black olives
1/2 cup capers
1 anchovy filet
2 cloves garlic, minced
1/4 cup chopped Italian flat leaf parsley
1/2 cup olive oil
Fresh cracked pepper to taste

Combine all ingredients in food processor and process until chunky. Serve at room temperature.

Wild Mushroom Jazz

8 ounces white mushrooms, sliced
8 ounces portabella mushrooms, sliced
8 ounces shiitake mushrooms, sliced
1-2 tablespoons flour
3-4 tablespoons butter, melted
1/4 cup chopped sun-dried tomatoes
3 tablespoons Marsala wine or Madeira wine

Sauté mushrooms in butter until soft. Add sun-dried tomatoes and flour. Cook until thick. Add wine and cook an additional 5-10 minutes.

Lamb Chop Lollipops

3 lbs. lamb chops (cut from a rack of lamb)
1 teaspoon kosher salt
1 teaspoon fresh cracked pepper
1 teaspoon garlic powder
1/4 cup olive oil

Sprinkle lamb chops with salt, pepper and garlic powder. Drizzle with 1/4 cup olive oil. Roast uncovered at 350º for 30-40 minutes.

Dijon Honey Sauce

1/2 cup honey
1 cup Dijon mustard
Dash of hot sauce

Whisk together ingredients. Serve chilled.

Spicy Mint Sauce

1 8-ounce jar mint jelly
2 tablespoons horseradish

Combine ingredients. Serve chilled.

How do you catch a falling knife? You don't! Step aside, let it drop and hope that the cat or dog is in the other room.

Food is an expression of love. As a matter of fact, I am always saying that love is a very important ingredient for a superb meal! Care about the people you are cooking for and your food will show it. In this busy world, a homecooked, lovingly prepared meal can be a peaceful and delightfully delicious experience. Show that someone special how much you care. Light the candles, buy some flowers, have dinner in a different part of the house. Share your love through glorious foods—it's rewarding for both of you and can create wonderful memories. Have a feast for lovers and keep the home fire burning!

Crab and Tomato Bisque

2 lbs. jumbo lump crabmeat
1 stick butter, melted
1 1/2 cups chopped onion
3 stalks celery, chopped
1 garlic clove, minced
2-3 tablespoons chopped Italian flat leaf parsley
1-2 tablespoons flour
1 tablespoon Old Bay seasoning
2 cups marinara sauce
2 quarts chicken broth
1 29-ounce can crushed tomatoes
Kosher salt and fresh cracked pepper to taste
1 teaspoon dried thyme
1/2 cup heavy cream or Half & Half
1 teaspoon Worcestershire sauce

Sauté onion, celery, garlic and parsley in butter until soft, about 10 minutes. Add flour and seafood seasoning and cook until mixture gets thick. Add marinara, chicken broth, tomatoes and crabmeat. Season with salt, pepper and thyme. Whisk in cream and Worcestershire before serving.

Madeira Mushrooms Sautéed with Sun-Dried Tomatoes

You can use this mushroom mixture in tiny phyllo tart shells for a delicious hors d'oeuvre. Fill tart shells with mixture and bake at 350º for 10-15 minutes.

1/2 cup sun-dried tomatoes, cut up
6 garlic cloves, minced
1/2 cup chopped Italian flat leaf parsley
2 shallots, chopped
1 stick butter
3 lbs. mushrooms, sliced
1/2 cup flour
Kosher salt and fresh cracked pepper to taste
1/2 cup Madeira wine
1 cup heavy cream

Sauté garlic, parsley, shallots and sun-dried tomatoes in 1/2 stick of butter. Add remaining butter and cook mushrooms. Stir in flour. Season with salt and pepper. Add Madeira wine and heavy cream. Reheat covered at 350º for 20-25 minutes.

Spring Salad with Orange Dressing and Carmelized Red Onion

Garnished with orange slices and sugared nuts, this salad makes a lovely presentation.

Orange Dressing

1 tablespoon Dijon mustard
2-3 garlic cloves
1 tablespoon honey
1/4 cup red wine vinegar
1/4 cup orange juice
1/2 cup grated Parmesan cheese
Kosher salt and fresh cracked pepper to taste
1 cup olive oil

Combine dressing ingredients in food processor.

Carmelized Red Onion

1 cup thinly sliced red onion
1 tablespoon brown sugar
1 tablespoon butter
orange slices (optional)
sugared nuts (optional)

Sauté onions in butter and brown sugar until golden. Drizzle dressing over greens and top with carmelized onion. Garnish with orange slices and sugared nuts.

"I love you." You can never say those words too much. I like to say that you will get what you give. It's important to say, "I love you" to the people in your life—not just on special occasions, but every day. It is a wonderful thing to be loved and appreciated. We need more love in all of our lives. So tell someone you love them, today and everyday. You'll get lots of love in return!

Set the Mood for Romance

Starlight to Candlelight

- Illuminate your table with soft lighting. Candles of different shapes and sizes create a wonderful glow, setting a romantic mood.
- Champagne goblets or unusual glasses set with votive candles create beautiful lighting. A touch of water in each glass will make them easy to clean. A single color holds the essence of the light together.

Set a Romantic Table for an Enchanted Evening

- Scatter rose petals across a dessert buffet setting.
- An inexpensive bolt of lace or netting purchased from a fabric store can be draped around your table.
- A favorite quilt or throw used as a table covering creates a beautiful country look.

Bring out the Silver and Crystal

- Dust off all those lovely presents you save for special occasions and use them. You will be glad you did!

Pistachio Crusted Salmon

1 side of salmon, skin removed (approx 3-3 1/2 lbs.)
1/2 cup olive oil
2 tablespoons honey
4 tablespoons Dijon mustard
4 cloves garlic, minced
2 teaspoons cayenne pepper
2 tablespoons lemon juice
Kosher salt and fresh cracked pepper to taste
1 cup crushed pistachio nuts
Fresh dill for garnish

Whisk together oil, honey, Dijon, garlic, cayenne pepper, lemon juice, salt and pepper. Pour over salmon and top with crushed pistachio nuts. Bake uncovered at 350º for 20-30 minutes. Use fresh dill for garnish. Serve at room temperature.

Pasta with Shrimp in Vodka Sauce

1/2 stick butter
4 cloves garlic, minced
6 plum tomatoes, chopped
2 tablespoons chopped Italian flat leaf parsley
2 tablespoons chopped fresh basil
1/4 cup vodka
Kosher salt and fresh cracked pepper to taste
1/2 cup heavy cream
Dash of hot sauce or red pepper flakes
2 lbs. frozen cooked and cleaned shrimp, defrosted and drained
1/4 cup chicken broth
1 lb. cooked pasta (reserve 1/4 cup pasta water)
1/4 cup grated Parmesan cheese

Sauté garlic in butter. Add tomatoes, parsley, basil and vodka. Season with salt and pepper. Add shrimp and remaining ingredients. Toss with 1 lb. cooked pasta and reserved pasta water. Sprinkle Parmesan cheese on top.

The two best tools you have when cooking are attached to you. They are your hands!

Chocolate Covered Strawberry Shortcake

2 pints strawberries
1/4 cup plus 2 tablespoons triple sec
2 tablespoons sugar
2 8-ounce packages cream cheese, softened
1/4 cup brown sugar
2 tablespoons Marsala wine
1 cup whipped cream
3 packages lady fingers
1 dozen chocolate covered strawberries

Combine strawberries, 1/4 cup triple sec and sugar. Set aside. Combine cream cheese, brown sugar, 2 tablespoons triple sec and Marsala wine in food processor and process until smooth. Layer ladyfingers, cream cheese mix and strawberry mixture. Repeat, finishing with whipped cream and chocolate covered strawberries.

Fresh whipped cream

1 1/2 cups heavy cream
1/4 cup powdered sugar
1 teaspoon instant vanilla pudding

To make fresh whipped cream, combine all ingredients in food processor. Process until thick and creamy. About 2-3 minutes.

Chocolate Covered Strawberries

To make chocolate covered strawberries, melt 1 1/2 cups chocolate chips. Mix until smooth. Dip strawberries in mixture and place in refrigerator to harden.

Mother's Day is a special day worth celebrating with all the women who are important to you—sisters, aunts, grandparents and neighbors. I host a Mother's Day luncheon every year. It's a time to bring everyone together in an atmosphere of appreciation and love, the two things we all need in our lives. Celebrate women. Gather your friends and family. Keep the menu simple and abundant. Remember, it's the thought that counts. Making memories with special gatherings is a great way to live your life. Relationships, love and people are what matter most. You share a part of yourself when you prepare a meal. Gather together and celebrate all the good that life holds for us.

Crab and Tomato Dip

You can use this crab and tomato mix to make delicious quesadillas.

- 2 cups shredded cheddar cheese
- 1/4 cup chopped Italian flat leaf parsley or cilantro
- 1 cup mayonnaise
- 1 cup chopped tomatoes
- 1 4.5-ounce can chopped chili
- 4 ounces cream cheese, softened
- 2 tablespoons orange or lime juice
- 1 lb. jumbo lump crabmeat
- 1/2 cup chopped scallions
- Dash of hot sauce

Combine ingredients and pour into an ovenproof casserole dish. Bake uncovered at 350º for 20-25 minutes. Serve with tortilla chips.

For quesadillas, fill a soft flour tortilla with 2-3 tablespoons of mixture. Fold tortilla in half. Brown both sides in a sauté pan until golden. Let cool. Slice into wedges and reheat uncovered at 350º for 10-15 minutes.

Shrimp Crostini

Cream Cheese Mixture

- 8 ounces cream cheese, softened
- 2 garlic cloves, minced
- 2 tablespoons olive oil

Sauté garlic in oil until fragrant. Remove from pan and combine with softened cream cheese.

Shrimp mixture

- 1 tablespoon capers
- 3 plum tomatoes, sliced
- 1 red or yellow pepper, diced
- 2 scallions, minced
- Kosher salt and fresh cracked pepper to taste
- 2 lbs. frozen cooked and cleaned shrimp, defrosted, drained and cut up

Combine ingredients. Spread cream cheese mixture on bread slices. Top with shrimp mixture. Serve cold.

Use a series of small bottles or teacups to hold bright, seasonal flowers. Set on mirrors.

"Feelin' Blue" Salad

Iceberg lettuce
4 plum tomatoes, diced
Reserved crumbled blue cheese

Dressing

1/2 lb. blue cheese, crumbled (reserve some for garnish)
1 teaspoon Worcestershire sauce
Dash of hot sauce
Kosher salt and fresh cracked pepper to taste
1 cup olive oil
1/4 cup mayonnaise

Combine dressing ingredients in food processor until smooth. Top lettuce with dressing, tomatoes and blue cheese.

Marinated Lemon Asparagus

2 lbs. asparagus, cooked
1/2 cup olive oil
2 cloves garlic, minced
1 lemon, sliced thin, seeds removed
Kosher salt and fresh cracked pepper to taste
1/4 cup grated Parmesan cheese

Boil or steam asparagus, 7-8 minutes. Sauté lemons and garlic in hot oil. Season with salt and pepper. Pour over asparagus. Sprinkle with Parmesan cheese. Serve at room temperature.

Carmelized Onion Bread Pudding

This is a delicious side dish!

1/2 stick butter, melted
3 cups thinly sliced onion
4 garlic cloves, chopped
Kosher salt and fresh cracked pepper to taste
5 large eggs
1/4 cup light corn syrup
1 tablespoon Worcestershire sauce
Dash of hot sauce
2 cups heavy cream
4 cups Italian bread slices
1 cup grated Parmesan cheese

Sauté onions and garlic in butter, uncovered, until golden, 10-15 minutes. Whisk together eggs, corn syrup, Worcestershire sauce, hot sauce and heavy cream. Layer bread slices in an ovenproof dish. Top with sautéed onions and pour liquid mix over onions and bread. Sprinkle with cheese. Bake uncovered at 350º for 30-40 minutes.

When breaking eggs into a bowl, a small bit of shell inevitably falls in. Instead of sticking your fingers in to fish it out, use the half of a cracked shell to scoop it up. It will act as a magnet and you'll have that eggshell out in a hurry!

Roasted Vegetables Antipasto

This is a tasty side dish. Serve at room temperature.

1 large eggplant (about 1 lb.), cut into chunks
4 cups zucchini, cut into chunks
1 yellow pepper, cut into strips
1 red pepper, cut into strips
1 1/2 cups chopped onion
1 cup chopped red onion
Kosher salt and fresh cracked pepper to taste
1/2 cup olive oil
1/2 lb. green beans
2-3 cloves garlic, minced
1 tablespoon capers

Toss vegetables with oil, capers, salt and pepper. Roast uncovered at 350º for 40-50 minutes, stirring occasionally. Serve at room temperature.

Honey Sesame Chicken

2-3 tablespoons butter
1 lb. boneless chicken breast, cut into scallops
1 cup soy sauce
3 cloves garlic, chopped
1 tablespoon chopped ginger
1/4 cup brown sugar
1/3 cup honey
1 tablespoon sesame oil
2-3 scallions, chopped

Sauté chicken in butter until golden on both sides. Remove and place in an ovenproof dish. In same saucepan, combine soy sauce, garlic, ginger, brown sugar, honey and sesame oil for 5-10 minutes. Pour over chicken scallops and bake covered at 350º for 20-25 minutes. Garnish with scallions.

Chocolate Espresso Sauce

This chocolate sauce is also delicious served over pound cake or ice cream.

1/2 cup brewed espresso coffee
2 cups whipping cream
2 tablespoons sugar
2 cups chocolate chips
1/2 cup butter
2 pints strawberries

Simmer espresso, whipping cream and sugar in saucepan until melted. Whisk in chocolate chips and butter until melted. Serve chilled over strawberries.

When a recipe calls for espresso coffee, you can substitute strongly brewed regular coffee.

Watermelon and Strawberry Margarita

Everyone will ask you for this recipe!

3 cups chopped seedless watermelon
3 cups chopped strawberries
2 cups tequila
1/2 cup lime juice
1 cup triple sec
1/2 cup sugar

Combine ingredients in blender. Served chilled.

Hosting a Tea is a perfect way to entertain for a bridal shower, baby shower or an afternoon with the girls—light and delicious. It can be fun and spur your creativity. Decorate your table with antique teapots filled with fresh flowers. Host the Tea in your garden and use terra cotta pots to hold scones, muffins or flatware and napkins. Polish that silver. Scour antique stores for wonderful linens. Create old world elegance with the ease of do ahead recipes. Votive candles in stemmed glasses can add a simple but elegant touch. Entertain with style and don't forget to have fun!

Open-Faced Watercress Sandwiches

You can make this cream cheese mixture two days ahead of time and assemble sandwiches on the morning of your party.

8 ounces cream cheese, softened
8 ounces butter
1/2 cup watercress
Kosher salt and pepper to taste
Grape tomatoes, halved for garnish
Bread slices from long rolls

Combine cream cheese, butter, watercress, salt and pepper in food processor. Spread mixture on bread slices and garnish with halved grape tomatoes.

Tea Sandwiches

1/2 cup whipped butter, softened
1 cup mayonnaise
1 cup blue cheese
1 lb. smoked turkey, sliced thin
12 slices soft white bread

Blend together mayonnaise and blue cheese. Spread softened butter on bread slices and then spread with blue cheese mixture. Top with turkey and cut into shapes.

Smoked Salmon Mousse on Cucumber Slices

2 8 ounce packages cream cheese, softened
1/4 cup heavy cream
2 scallions, minced
1 teaspoon lemon juice
Dash of hot sauce
6 ounces smoked salmon
2-3 cucumbers, sliced 1 inch thick

Chop smoked salmon in food processor. Remove and set aside salmon and DO NOT clean processor. Add cream cheese, heavy cream, lemon juice, scallions and hot sauce to processor. Combine. Remove from processor and gently fold in with salmon. Pipe salmon mousse on cucumber slices.

You can use a plastic food storage bag to pipe mixture onto cucumbers. Fill the bag with mixture, cut off one corner of the bag, and lightly squeeze out the mousse.

English Tea Cinnamon Scones

- 4 cups flour
- 4 teaspoons baking powder
- 1 teaspoon kosher salt
- 1/2 teaspoon cream of tartar
- 1/4 cup sugar
- 2/3 cup butter, chilled
- 1 1/2 cups light cream
- 1 large egg
- 2 tablespoons sugar
- 1 tablespoon cinnamon sugar

Combine flour, baking powder, salt, cream of tartar and sugar. Blend butter into dry mix by hand until crumbly. Combine cream and egg, then blend into crumbly mixture. Set aside and let rest 5-10 minutes. Blend together 2 tablespoons sugar and cinnamon. Pat out dough into 3/4 inch thickness. Cut into circles. Brush with 1/2 cup milk. Sprinkle with cinnamon sugar. Bake uncovered at 350º for 15-20 minutes.

Apricot Chutney

- 1 1/2 cups apricot preserves
- 1/3 cup rice vinegar
- 1/3 cup Dijon mustard
- 1 teaspoon minced ginger
- 1 teaspoon brown sugar
- 8 ounces cream cheese, softened

Combine all ingredients and heat until thick, 8-10 minutes. Cool. Pour over softened cream cheese. Serve with crackers.

Ham and Cheddar Muffins

- 1 cup finely chopped ham
- 3 tablespoons butter, melted
- 1 medium onion, chopped fine
- 1 1/2 cups baking mix
- 2 cups shredded cheddar cheese
- 1/2 cup milk
- 1 large egg

Beat egg and milk together. Cook ham and onion in sauté pan until soft, 5-10 minutes. Combine egg mixture, baking mix and cheese with ham and onion mixture and put into greased muffin pans. Bake uncovered at 350º for 20 minutes or until golden.

Luscious Bars

- 1 1/2 cups graham cracker crumbs
- 1/2 cup butter, melted
- 1 cup flaked coconut
- 1 14-ounce can sweetened condensed milk
- 1 1/2 cups chocolate chips
- 1/2 cup peanut butter

In saucepan, melt together chocolate chips and peanut butter. Set aside. Spread butter in 13 x 9 baking pan and sprinkle with graham cracker crumbs. Top with coconut and condensed milk. Bake at 350º for 20 minutes until golden. While still hot, drizzle with melted chocolate and peanut butter mixture. Let cool. Cut into squares.

Tasty Tapas

I first had the pleasure of dining in a Tapas restaurant in Amsterdam, a city with a different approach to life. Amsterdam has an array of restaurants. We wandered into the Tapas bar and were in for a wild and crazy ride! Not really knowing what we were ordering, we let our adventurous nature take over. We sat at a tiny corner table listening to flamenco music, people watching and enjoying the extravaganza of tiny tasting that I will never forget. Little terra cotta plates, each holding a specialty bursting with flavor, were presented to us in a slow, steady rhythm. We were in heaven, sampling and enjoying—it is a wonderful way to eat. Have a Tapas party and surprise your guests with different flavors and fabulous music.

Herb Oil

1 sprig fresh rosemary
1 sprig fresh oregano
2 bay leaves
Fresh cracked pepper to taste
1 1/2 cups olive oil

Combine all ingredients in a shallow fancy dish. Serve with bread slices.

Good quality olive oil really makes a difference. Try different brands. The darker and greener the olive oil, the fruitier the flavor.

Marinated Olives

8 ounces green olives
8 ounces black olives

Marinade

1 tablespoon chopped Italian flat leaf parsley
1-2 teaspoons dried chili flakes
Dash of lemon juice
1 tablespoon red wine vinegar
10 cloves garlic, crushed
1-2 bay leaves
Fresh cracked pepper to taste
2 tablespoons olive oil

Combine marinade ingredients and toss with olives. Allow to sit 1-2 hours prior to serving.

Roasted Peppers

The perfect accompaniment to a platter of sharp cheese.

3-4 peppers, charred, peeled and cut up
3 tablespoons olive oil
1 tablespoon chopped Italian flat leaf parsley
2 cloves garlic, chopped
Kosher salt and fresh cracked pepper to taste

Combine all ingredients. Serve at room temperature.

Marinated Goat Cheese

8 ounces goat cheese, crumbled
1-2 cloves garlic, chopped
1/4 cup chopped Italian flat leaf parsley
1/4 cup chopped sun-dried tomatoes
1/2 cup olive oil
Kosher salt and fresh cracked pepper to taste

Gently toss garlic, parsley and sun-dried tomatoes in oil. Add salt and pepper to taste. Pour over crumbled goat cheese. Serve with bread slices.

Potato Salad

6-8 potatoes, diced into 1/4 inch pieces and cooked
1/2 cup chopped carrots
1/2 cup frozen peas, defrosted
1 cup mayonnaise
Dash of cayenne pepper
Kosher salt and fresh cracked pepper to taste
1 tablespoon chopped Italian flat leaf parsley
1 tablespoon Dijon mustard
1 teaspoon honey

Combine mayonnaise with Dijon, honey and seasoning. Toss with peas, carrots and potatoes.

Always boil potatoes in unsalted water unless making mashed potatoes. Unsalted water keeps the potatoes firmer. Adding salt to the water breaks up the potatoes and makes them easier to mash.

Mushrooms in Garlic and Parsley

Madeira wine, Marsala wine or white vermouth can be substituted for the vermouth in this recipe.

1/4 cup olive oil
2-3 garlic cloves, whole or sliced
1 lb. mushrooms, sliced
2 tablespoons chopped Italian flat leaf parsley
Kosher salt and fresh cracked pepper
1 tablespoon flour
1/4 cup dark vermouth

Sauté garlic in hot oil. Add mushrooms and parsley. Season with salt and pepper. Sprinkle with flour and cook until absorbed. Add vermouth and cook until thick. If mixture gets too thick, add more vermouth.

Roasted Sweet Potatoes with Salsa

1 lb. sweet potatoes, cut into 1/4 inch rounds
1/4 cup olive oil
2 garlic cloves, chopped
Kosher salt and fresh cracked pepper

Mix olive oil, garlic, salt and pepper and toss with potatoes. Roast uncovered at 350º for 20 minutes.

Cilantro Salsa

1/4 cup chopped cilantro
1 teaspoon red pepper flakes
1 garlic clove, minced
6-8 tablespoons olive oil
1 tablespoon lime juice
1/2 teaspoon ground cumin
Kosher salt and fresh cracked pepper to taste

Combine ingredients for salsa. Layer roasted potatoes in a platter and spoon salsa on top. Serve at room temperature.

Baked Eggs

1 cup marinara sauce
1 teaspoon hot sauce
6-8 eggs
1/2 cup grated Parmesan cheese
1/4 cup chopped chives

Seasoned Bread Crumbs

2 garlic cloves, chopped
1/4 cup olive oil
2 cups bread crumbs
1/2 cup grated Parmesan cheese

Mix marinara sauce with hot sauce. Pour into an 8-inch or larger round ovenproof pottery dish. Break eggs into marinara - do not disturb yolk. Combine ingredients for breadcrumbs. Top egg mixture with grated cheese, chives and seasoned bread crumbs. Bake covered at 350º until eggs are set. Uncover for 5 minutes to brown top. Serve with bread for dipping.

Spanish Omelet

3-4 tablespoons olive oil
5 potatoes, thinly sliced
1 large onion, thinly sliced
Kosher salt and fresh cracked pepper to taste
12 eggs

Sauté onions with potatoes in oil until golden, 10-15 minutes. Season with salt and pepper. Pour into a large ovenproof dish. Beat eggs until foamy, then pour over potatoes and onions. Bake covered at 350º for 15-20 minutes or until eggs are set. Serve warm.

Meatballs

1 lb. ground mix (beef, pork and veal)
1/2 cup finely chopped onion
4 cloves garlic, minced
1 tablespoon chopped Italian flat leaf parsley
1 cup fresh breadcrumbs
3 eggs
Dash of chili sauce
Kosher salt and fresh cracked pepper to taste

Mix ingredients. Fry meatballs in vegetable oil, turning to brown both sides. Drain well. Serve with toothpicks. Can be prepared in advance and reheated when needed.

Garlic Spicy Shrimp

1/2 cup olive oil
8 cloves garlic, chopped
1 teaspoon red pepper flakes
1 teaspoon seafood seasoning
1 teaspoon hot sauce
1/2 cup white wine
Kosher salt and fresh cracked pepper to taste
1 tablespoon chopped Italian flat leaf parsley
2-3 lbs. frozen cooked shrimp, defrosted and drained

Sauté garlic, red pepper flakes, seasoning and hot sauce in oil. Add wine and remaining ingredients. Toss with shrimp. Serve at room temperature.

Spicy Spanish Chicken Skewers

1 lb. boneless chicken breast, sliced into strips
6-inch bamboo skewers

Thread chicken strips on bamboo skewers. Layer on cookie sheet and bake uncovered at 350º for 15-20 minutes. Remove and place on pretty platter.

Spicy Spanish Sauce

2 tablespoons olive oil
2 cloves garlic, chopped
2 teaspoons chopped ginger
1 large onion, chopped
1 teaspoon cumin
1 teaspoon paprika
1 teaspoon cayenne pepper
1 13.5-ounce can coconut milk
Kosher salt and fresh cracked pepper to taste
1 tablespoon brown sugar

Sauté ginger, garlic and onion in hot oil. Add seasonings, coconut milk and brown sugar. Use as dipping sauce with cooked chicken skewers.

This versatile sauce can be used for beef skewers or shrimp and vegetable kabobs.

Chile Scallops

3 lbs. scallops
1/2 cup flour
2-3 tablespoons olive oil
2 tablespoons butter
1 teaspoon brown sugar
1 tablespoon chopped garlic
1 teaspoon chopped ginger
1 tablespoon chopped cilantro
1 tablespoon hot sauce
1 teaspoon sesame oil
1 tablespoon soy sauce
1 teaspoon sesame seeds
1/4 cup water
Kosher salt and fresh cracked pepper to taste

Rinse scallops and dry with paper towel, then lightly flour. Sauté scallops in oil and butter until golden. Remove and put in ovenproof pottery dish. Combine remaining ingredients in the same saucepan. Cook until fragrant, about 5-10 minutes. Pour over scallops.

Barbecued Sliced Filet

1 whole filet roast (5-7 lbs.)

Season with salt, pepper, oil and garlic powder. Roast uncovered at 350º until internal temperature reaches 155º, about 1-1 1/2 hours. Cool and slice.

Barbecue Sauce

1 cup ketchup
1/2 cup Dijon mustard
1 tablespoon brown sugar
1 teaspoon Worcestershire sauce
1 teaspoon hot sauce
1/2 cup water
Kosher salt and fresh cracked pepper to taste

Combine sauce ingredients in saucepan and heat to blend. Pour over cooked and sliced filet.

You can also serve this sauce on the side at room temperature as an accompaniment to the sliced filet.

Spanish Sangria

8 cups red wine
1/2 cup sugar
1/2 cup triple sec
2 pints berries, sliced
1/2 cup brandy
1 quart lemon lime soda
1 lemon, sliced
1 orange, sliced

Combine all ingredients. Serve chilled.

A wonderful time to entertain, brunch also offers a chance to be with family and friends while still having the evening to relax. Much of your menu can be prepared in advance, allowing you the opportunity to enjoy your own celebration. Foods can be light and colorful. The table decorations can reflect your theme. Gather old coffee mugs and fill them with flowers. Sprinkle coffee beans on your table and flavor your orange juice with champagne. A brunch is ideal for holiday entertaining when everyone is so busy and booked with nighttime events. It is a special way to reminisce the day after a wedding. Try this easy and fabulous theme for your next party.

Gorgonzola and Roasted Red Pepper Bruschetta

1 cup crumbled gorgonzola or blue cheese
4 peppers, roasted and peeled
2 tablespoons olive oil
1 tablespoon chopped Italian flat leaf parsley
Kosher salt and fresh crack pepper to taste
Italian rolls, sliced

To roast peppers, place them on direct flame either in a broiler or on the barbecue grill. Blacken peppers and put them into a paper bag until they cool - this will allow the steam to soften the skin. When cool, peel off charred, blackened skin. Scrape out seeds and cut up peppers. Toss peppers with salt, pepper, oil and parsley. Layer on bread slices and top with crumbled cheese. Serve at room temperature.

Asparagus and Orange Salad over Greens with Orange Vinaigrette

3 cups cut up asparagus
2 large oranges, peeled and sliced
Bed of lettuce
1 red onion, thinly sliced
1/2 cup sliced almonds, toasted

Vinaigrette

1/2 cup olive oil
1 tablespoon red wine vinegar
1 tablespoon orange juice
1 teaspoon orange preserves
1 teaspoon sugar
Kosher salt and fresh cracked pepper to taste

Boil or steam asparagus, cooking until tender, 5-7 minutes. Combine vinaigrette ingredients in food processor until thick, 2-3 minutes. Layer greens, red onion, asparagus and oranges. Pour dressing over salad and sprinkle with toasted nuts.

To toast nuts, place nuts on a cookie sheet and bake at 350º for 10-15 minutes, stirring occasionally. Watch the nuts - they burn easily.

Smoked Salmon and Goat Cheese Torte

6 tablespoons butter
1 shallot, chopped
1 cup chopped smoked salmon
1 cup crumbled goat cheese
1/4 cup flour
1 1/4 cup milk, warmed
4 large eggs
2 teaspoons chopped dill
Kosher salt and fresh cracked pepper to taste

Sauté shallots in 2 tablespoons melted butter. Add salmon. In baking dish, layer salmon and shallots and sprinkle with goat cheese. In 4 tablespoons melted butter, add flour to make a roux. It will become a golden paste. (This takes 5-10 minutes.) Add warmed milk and whisk until thick. Add beaten eggs and seasoning. Pour over cheese and salmon. Garnish with dill. Bake uncovered at 350º for 30-35 minutes or until golden brown.

Pasta with Spicy Lobster Sauce

Purchase cooked lobster meat at your local seafood market.

2 lbs. lobster tails, steamed
2-3 garlic cloves, minced
1 teaspoon red pepper flakes
1 teaspoon seafood seasoning
2 cups marinara sauce
1 tablespoon chopped basil
1 teaspoon dried tarragon
1/4 cup light cream
2 tablespoons butter
2 tablespoons olive oil
1 lb. cooked pasta (reserve 1/4 cup pasta water)

Remove lobster meat from steamed tails and cut into chunks. Sauté lobster, garlic, red pepper flakes, basil, tarragon and seafood seasoning in oil and butter. Cook until fragrant, 10-15 minutes. Add marinara and light cream along with reserved pasta water. Toss with cooked pasta.

Apricot Almond French Toast

6 large eggs
1/2 cup heavy cream
1 teaspoon vanilla extract
20 slices French bread or bread cut from an Italian roll
2 tablespoons butter
2 tablespoons vegetable oil
8 ounces cream cheese
2 cups apricot preserves
1/4 cup amaretto liqueur
1/2 cup sliced almonds

Mix together eggs, cream and vanilla extract. Dip bread slices in egg mixture. Sauté both sides in butter and oil. Layer half of the bread slices in ovenproof pottery dish. Top each slice with a dollop of cream cheese. Repeat with the remaining slices. In saucepan, heat together preserves, amaretto and almonds. Spread apricot mixture over bread and bake at 350º for 15-20 minutes.

Change old patterns and habits. Take a different way home from work or shop at a different store. We go through life on remote control, not even noticing what is around us. Have you ever left your house and gotten to your destination without knowing how? We need to pay attention to our surroundings and take pleasure in everything that we do. Mix it up a little! You'll be surprised at how good it feels.

Ask for help. Many of us feel we need to do everything by ourselves, on our own. We have family and friends offering help and we brush them away. Try saying yes to a friend who offers to help. It is a gift for them as well as yourself.

Cook with friends. Instead of preparing for a dinner party alone, invite your guests to help. You will have much laughter in the kitchen and your guests will never forget your party.

Life is too short to waste on a bad meal!

Communication is an important part of life. When we hold things in, we are creating havoc with our mind, our heart and our health. If you are angry or sad, take a deep breath. Clarify what is bothering you and talk it out with the other person. It releases all that bad energy that makes us feel so helpless. Get it off your chest and you will feel so much better.

APPETIZERS

SOUPS, STEWS AND CHOWDERS

SALADS AND DRESSINGS

MAIN ENTRÉES

PASTA

SEAFOOD

ITALIAN COUNTRYSIDE

SIDE DISHES

DAZZLING DESSERTS

DRINKS AND PUNCHES

COMFORT FOODS

KIDS' FOOD

ASIAN INFLUENCES

"HOT STUFF" GRILLING

GIVING THANKS

A TASTING PARTY

A FEAST FOR LOVERS

MOTHER'S DAY LUNCH

TEA TIME

TASTY TAPAS

BRUNCH

Stock Your Kitchen

SELECTIONS OF PASTA
- orzo of riso
- ditalini
- penne
- far falle (bow ties)
- fedilini

REFRIGERATOR
- mayonnaise
- Italian flat leaf parsley
- capers
- carrots
- celery
- scallions
- mushrooms
- ginger
- lemons
- basil
- sun-dried tomatoes
- butter
- light cream
- half & half
- Parmesan cheese
- marinara sauce
- cream cheese
- pork tenderloins
- boneless chicken
- bacon
- lemon juice
- lime juice
- jumbo lump crabmeat

FREEZER
- peas
- shrimp
- spinach (frozen chopped)
- frozen fruit

OTHER GOODS
- chicken broth
- beef broth
- clam broth
- dark vermouth
- white vermouth
- Marsala wine
- plum tomatoes (canned)
- canned beans (white, red, black)
- cream of corn, chicken, celery and mushroom soups
- olive oil
- blended oil or vegetable oil
- canned corn
- honey
- soy or teriyaki sauce
- hot sauce
- kosher Salt
- fresh cracked pepper
- balsamic vinegar
- shallots
- red potatoes
- onions
- garlic
- red onions

TOOLS
- pepper mill
- mandolin
- sharp knives
- food processor
- sauté pans
- heat resistant spatula